WONDERFUL AND DARK IS THIS ROAD

Books by Emilie Griffin

Turning: Reflections on the Experience of Conversion

Clinging: the Experience of Prayer

Pope John Paul II Visits the City of New Orleans
(with William Griffin)

Chasing the Kingdom: a Parable of Faith

Once Upon a Christmas

The Reflective Executive: a Spirituality of Business and Enterprise

Homeward Voyage: Reflections on Life Changes

Wilderness Time: a Guide for Spiritual Retreat

Spiritual Classics: Readings for Individuals and Groups
(with Richard J. Foster)

These Sisters Are My Friends:
A Brief History of the Eucharistic Missionaries of St. Dominic

Doors into Prayer: an Invitation

Evelyn Underhill: Essential Writings

Epiphanies: Stories for the Christian Year
(with Eugene Peterson)

WONDERFUL AND DARK IS THIS ROAD

Discovering the Mystic Path

Emilie Griffin

PARACLETE PRESS

BREWSTER, MASSACHUSETTS

Library of Congress Cataloging-in-Publication Data

Griffin, Emilie.
Wonderful and dark is this road : discovering the mystic path / Emilie Griffin.
   p. cm.
ISBN 1-55725-358-7 (pbk.)
1. Mysticism. I. Title.
BV5082.3.G75 2004
248.2'2–dc22   2004002076

10 9 8 7 6 5 4 3 2 1

© 2004 by Emilie Griffin

ISBN 1-55725-358-7

Published by Paraclete Press
Brewster, Massachusetts
www.paracletepress.com
Printed in the United States of America.

About mysticism: why are people wary of the word? Too strong? It is what it is.

—*John Williams to Emilie Griffin, via e-mail,
entitled "Mysticism and . . ." dated October 7, 2001*

✎ CONTENTS

✒ ACKNOWLEDGMENTS

I want to thank my husband William Griffin, a writer and scholar, for his unfailing support and assistance to me in the completion of this book. I must mention, gratefully, the support of Lillian Miao and Lil Copan at Paraclete. My thanks go to Margaret Campbell, who was kind enough to read early drafts of some chapters. I am grateful to Fr. Harvey D. Egan, S.J., whose work on the mystics I have followed over several decades, and to Dana Greene, an authority on Evelyn Underhill, who has recently encouraged me in my Underhill work. Though I am not acquainted with either Bernard or Patricia McGinn, I must acknowledge my deep debt to them as dedicated scholars of Christian mysticism. I also want to thank Warren Farha, my good friend and colleague, who made many fine suggestions of books and resources I might consult. John Williams, who died last summer, was a friend to me during my lifelong exploration of mysticism. I recently learned that he was a Fellow of King's College, London. My thanks go to Hannah Williams Parry and Victoria Williams Burman, who have kindly permitted me to quote a fragment of my correspondence with their father. Finally, I would mention my lifelong friend Paul Marechal, who is known as Brother Elias in the Cistercian community at Conyers, Georgia. He has been an inspiration to me in the pursuit of contemplative life.

Emilie Griffin
Alexandria, Louisiana
Feast of the Epiphany 2004

CHAPTER ONE

What is Mysticism?

hy do mystics seem rare and strange? To the rest of us they appear to live at the edge of existence. If pressed, we might name a few of them: John of the Cross, Francis of Assisi, Julian of Norwich. Mostly, they appear to be not of our place and time. We connect them with medieval and renaissance life, hardly recognizing that modern life also has mystics. No doubt most of these are unknown, anonymous. But a few names come to mind: Padre Pio, Simone Weil, Edith Stein. What do these modern figures have to tell us?

Out of reverence, perhaps, or respect, we have put "the mystics" on an exalted plane. Perhaps we do not really believe in them, for we find no such persons within our immediate circle. There may be other reasons to steer clear of them.

1

We have heard that mysticism is connected with unusual phenomena, the stigmata or "wounds of Christ," healing powers, levitation, "reading hearts," and still more startling effects. It is said that certain mystics have been seen in two places at one time! But such odd stories should not distract us. This study will not dwell on the strange and bizarre. Instead, we will explore the mystic path, that is, the recognized stages of the mystical journey.

In considering the mystic path, these questions come to mind. Are we expected to be mystics? What does mysticism have to do with the likes of us?

What is Mysticism?

Mysticism is a phenomenon that occurs in all of the world's religions in which practitioners of the spiritual life lay claim to a special intimacy with the Godhead; or, in the event that their religion lacks any idea of God, a special kind of enlightenment. We will concentrate on Christian mysticism, but will take into account some parallels in other great world religions and explore their influences on the Christian mystic path.[1]

A mystic is a person far advanced in the spiritual life, one who very likely spends time in prayer and worship with a disciplined regularity. But surely, this definition would include a fairly large number of people? Yet few receive the title of mystic. Just how is this title assigned? Even within such highly formalized structures as the Roman Catholic Church, no official procedure exists for naming or singling out mystics. The title of "mystic" is awarded by an informal consensus, a common opinion. Historically, the term "mystic" is drawn from the Greek word *mystos* (*mustes*), which means, *one who has special knowledge.* The term is applied to someone remarkable. In short, the mystical life is not only spiritual; it is also mysterious. It seems to lie beyond everyday experience. To make any account of it we must rely on what is said by the mystics themselves as well as observations and interpretations made about them.

A mystic is one who has observable symptoms of an unusual spirituality (such as dreams, visions, prophecies, or spiritual gifts) or one who gives personal testimony to encounters with with Jesus or Mary, or with God the Father, or with divine emissaries like angels or saints.

Joan of Arc is known as a mystic because of her divine visitors. This simple, fifteenth-century, French farm girl had an intense prayer life; she claimed to receive visits from the Archangel Michael, St. Margaret and other holy persons. Her saintly visitors gave her direct instructions to save France from the English; to present herself to the Dauphin and there to offer to lead armies against these English invaders. Hebrew prophets, especially Ezekiel, seem rooted in this transforming communion with God, which is also suggested by several psalms (Ps. 73:23–26 is one instance).[2]

In the earliest days of Christianity, Saul of Tarsus, a devout Jew who was attempting to stamp out Christian belief, received a vision of Jesus on the Damascus Road. As a result he experienced temporary blindness. His story is told in the Acts of the Apostles. Changed by his experience, Saul, later called Paul, became a Christian and devoted his life to spreading belief in Jesus as the Messiah.

The twentieth-century mystic, Padre Pio (1887–1968), received the stigmata. These unexplained open wounds appeared on his body in 1910 and remained until some months before his death, more than fifty years later. A simple Capuchin friar of peasant background, he lived in a monastery in the Apulian region of southern Italy and drew a large following among the faithful. Yet Padre Pio had a certain natural anonymity. It was difficult to pick him out in a crowd of his fellow-monks. Genuine mystics are not headline seekers. The glare of publicity that comes to them is a burden. Padre Pio found this to be true.

This simple monk was reported to have unusual insight. In 1947, when he heard the confession of a young Polish priest named Karol Wojtyla, he made the surprising claim that this young man would one day become Pope. As a confessor he was also said to have the gift of "reading hearts," knowing the secrets of penitents without being told, and without any prior knowledge of them. Also, he is reported to have had physical struggles with demons which left him bruised and bloodied. The stir caused by Padre Pio's gifts brought him a great deal of embarrassment and pain. Vatican experts who were investigating his case concluded that his wounds were brought about by psychological stress. These experts instructed him to stop saying Mass for a number of years. Padre Pio died in 1968 and was beatified by the Roman Catholic Church in 1999. He has since been declared a saint.[3]

When and How Did It All Begin?

Throughout human history certain persons have experienced closeness to God. This intimacy is manifested in many ways: confidence in God's love and power; courage to dialogue with God; willingness to engage in a kind of friendship with the Almighty; fondness for intense prayer and worship; and an effort to discern and carry out the divine will.

Looked at from a certain angle, biblical history is simply an account of such persons. To say that Adam heard God's commands suggests that Adam knew God directly. The relationship between God and Adam, before the Fall at least, was straightforward and immediate, mystical. Noah by divine message, was told to build an ark, to gather in the species two by two; all of which suggests that Noah was a mystic, too. Abraham's mysticism is easier to trace, for in Genesis 17:1 it is said that the Lord appears to Abram and says to him: "I am God Almighty; walk before me, and be blameless. And I will make my covenant between me and you, and will make you exceedingly numerous." One effect of this encounter is that Abram's name was changed to Abraham, and his wife Sarai became Sarah. Abraham prays intensely, even falling into trances on occasion. He receives direct commands from God—to leave his home and go to a far country; to build a nation, to sacrifice his son Isaac (and at the last minute, not to sacrifice him). In Genesis 15:1 "the word of the Lord came to Abram in a vision: 'Do not be afraid, Abram, I am your shield, your reward shall be very great.'" Later on, in Genesis 15:12, Abraham experiences a kind of trance or swoon: "As the sun was going down, a deep sleep fell upon Abram, and a deep and terrifying darkness descended upon him." In this darkness the Lord speaks and lets Abram know the future: that his descendants will be aliens in a land that is not theirs, and he receives other predictions which form the foundation of Abram's (and later Judeo-Christian) understanding. In the Abram-Abraham account God communicates plainly to others, as well. In Genesis 16:7 the slave-girl Hagar who has borne a son to Abram, runs away because of harsh treatment by Abram's wife Sarai. How is this conflict resolved? Through an angelic message. "The angel of the Lord found her by a spring of water in the wilderness, the spring on the way to Shur. And he said, 'Hagar, slave-girl of Sarai, where have you come from and where are you going?'" When she admits that she is running away from her mistress Sarai, the angel of the Lord bids her to return and submit to Sarai's discipline, because the Lord has rewards in store. It seems that women, if not the social equals of men, are equally favored by God's messengers.

In Genesis 18 Abraham bargains with God for the survival of the city of Sodom, in spite of its large population of evil-doers.

Such a friendship with God, in which Abraham feels free to negotiate with the Almighty (some suggest that he only wanted to trace the outlines of divine justice) implies a mystic's knowledge. Jacob's ladder—a revelation of angels—occurs in a dream. "And he dreamed that there was a ladder set up on the earth, the top of it reaching to heaven; and the angels of God were ascending and descending on it" (Gen. 28:12). This experience is widely interpreted as a revelation, a mystical encounter. So, too, is Jacob's meeting with the man-angel (Gen. 32:24). Jacob wrestles with God's messenger on the road, and, prevailing, receives a new name: Israel. In all this, the patriarchs—Abraham, Isaac and Jacob—are not only finding God but being found by him, responding to a divine initiative.

In short, the Bible describes and traces many mystical encounters between God and outstanding individuals in religious history. But the word "mystic" is not a biblical word. It is perhaps a scholar's word, a term applied by an outside observer who wants to explain claims to divine intimacy, to interpret and describe the encounter with God.

"The word *mystica* came into Christianity by way of the famous late fifth-century Syrian monk, Pseudo-Dionysius, who wrote a mystical classic, *Mystica Theologia*," notes Harvey Egan, a contemporary scholar of mysticism. Egan says that for Pseudo-Dionysius, "mysticism involved the . . . state of consciousness which experiences God as a ray of divine darkness." This monk, whose identity is obscure, wrote about 500 AD. He was influenced by both Greek Neoplatonists and Cappadocians. He is called "Pseudo" because he adopts the identity (a sort of *nom de plume,* not an unusual practice in his time) of a much earlier figure, Dionysius the Areopagite mentioned in Acts 17:34. C. S. Lewis (1898-1963) notes that for centuries this Dionysius was thought (wrongly) to be the one who was converted by Paul at the Areopagus. Lewis states: "His writings are generally regarded as the main channel by which a certain kind of theology entered the western tradition. It is the 'negative theology' of those who take in a more rigid sense, and emphasize more persistently, the incomprehensibility of God."[4] Lewis goes on to observe that this incomprehensibility of God "is already well rooted in Plato himself" and he finds it central to Plotinus.[5]

Dionysius is the first to use the term "mystical theology." Because his terminology is Greek, it is perhaps tempting to suppose that mysticism arises out of a confluence of Greek and Jewish experience and thought. As we shall see, however, the experience of mysticism is wider than any one culture or nation.

Although "mystic" is not a biblical word, Egan takes note of the Greek term *mysterion* (mystery) which is used in the New Testament, signifying "what many today consider mysticism to involve: the hidden presence of God and Christ in Scripture, the sacraments, and the events of daily life." Many early Christian theologians saw a mystical dimension in *exegesis* (scriptural close reading and interpretation) which became a kind of contemplation of the presence of Christ. Egan defines mysticism as "the universal thrust of the human spirit for experiential union with the Absolute and the theory of that union."

Surely Thomas Merton (1915–1968) has done a great deal to interpret mysticism to a broad modern audience. "Mysticism will probably always be a disturbing subject," Thomas Merton writes in his introduction to William Johnston's volume, *The Mysticism of the Cloud of Unknowing*.[6] "First of all the concept of mystical experience is easily misunderstood. Aberrations have been palmed off as true mysticism. Or the word has been defined so loosely and with so little respect for truth that mystical experience has been confused with every kind of emotional, pseudo-religious, aesthetic or supposedly extrasensory perception."

"Even when properly understood, and treated with perfect orthodoxy," Merton continues, "mysticism tends to inspire apprehension even in religious minds. Why? Because the mystic must surrender to a power of love that is greater than human and advance toward God in a darkness that goes beyond the light of reason and of human conceptual knowledge. Furthermore, there is no infallible way of guaranteeing the mystic against every mistake. . . . Only the grace of God can protect him and guide him."[7]

Is Merton right in thinking that mystics disturb us because we are confused about mysticism? Possibly, but another explanation comes to mind. Mystics may seem rare and strange to us precisely because they have given themselves to God so completely, as we ourselves lack the courage to do. Are they like us or different from us? Are we, too, called to follow the mystic path? Many of us, who see ourselves as "ordinary people," may nevertheless find ourselves unaccountably attracted by descriptions of the mystical life.

A BEWILDERING VARIETY

Mysticism, according to Thomas Corbishley in *The New Catholic Encyclopedia*, "is a term used to cover a literally bewildering variety of states of mind." Corbishley cites Jean Gerson's useful definition: "Mystical theology is knowledge of God by experience, arrived at through the embrace of unifying love." (Gerson, 1363–1429, was chancellor of the University of Paris, a noted theologian, spiritual writer and a recognized mystic.)

Three points should be considered, Corbishley suggests. First, mystical theology[8] differs from natural theology, which allows us to know God by reason, and from dogmatic theology, which allows us to know God through his revelation and word. Second, mystical theology is a further way of knowing

8

God. Third, this knowledge is not intellectual in nature. It comes to us through an experience of "unifying love."

How do mystics come to know God through such an experience? What precisely does this knowing involve? The Dominican scholar and philosopher Thomas Aquinas (1225–1274) provides a good explanation. Human knowledge begins with sense awareness: the color of the sky, the shapes of trees and houses, sights, sounds, feelings, perceptions of every kind. Out of all this sense data the intellect begins to devise abstract concepts, working from the lower world of change towards the upper realm of the Unchanging. From such abstract ideas the mind makes judgments, schemes, logical arguments, inferences. Ideas crystallize in our minds and we reach for words to express them.

In the highest forms of intellectual activity, images seem to get in our way. We try to move beyond them. In mathematics and geometry this hindrance of the image becomes obvious. The drawings, the formulas, the sketches are never the idea itself, and the mind wants to leap beyond sense-experience to some other realm of truth.

Our natures, Aquinas says, are finite and flawed. They are incapable of grasping the truth directly and immediately except through divine help. We have lost the special intimacy that Adam and Eve had before the Fall. We must rely on God—through special circumstances and the offering of divine favors—to lift the veil and invite us beyond the senses, beyond the intellect, far beyond. Thomas suggests a way beyond, and like most interpreters of mysticism, speaks of contemplation:

"In contemplation, God is seen by a medium which is the light of wisdom elevating the mind to discern the divine. . . . and thus the divine is seen by the contemplative by means of grace after sin, though more perfectly in the state of innocence."[9]

There is another important factor. The mystic, who has gone beyond ordinary knowledge, beyond intellectual ways of arriving at knowledge, <u>finds it hard to report to others what precisely has been learned or seen.</u> Augustine of Hippo expresses this difficulty: "Your invisible things, which I really saw, I could not however fix my gaze on. In my weakness I was pushed back, and I fell back on my ordinary experience."[10]

So it is that mystics in their efforts to describe a special knowledge granted to them, begin to take up unusual and poetic forms of description. Psalm 139 expresses their sense of inadequacy: "Such knowledge is too great for me. . . ." Mystical writers throughout the centuries rely on poetic figures to express a realm of higher consciousness which they claim as a direct revelation of the divine. They choose metaphors such as *The Interior Castle, The Living Flame of Love, The Cloud of Unknowing.*

Henry Vaughan (1621–1695) is one of many poets who have described a kind of mystical knowledge:

> I saw eternity the other night
> Like a great ring of pure and endless light
>   As calm as it was bright;
> And round beneath it, time, in hours, days, years,
>   Driven by the spheres,
> Like a vast shadow moved, in which the world
> And all her train were hurled.[11]

In ordinary experience, one does not *see*, but only conceives of, eternity. Vaughan lays claim to a religious knowledge that goes beyond the ordinary. In making such a claim, he is not alone.

Mysticism, as we have seen, is an important strand in Judeo-Christian history, a strand that weaves through the revealed word of God and continues in later times. Yet Christians and Jews have no monopoly on mysticism. Just as the experience of ancient Israel is somehow linked with Egyptian and Babylonian religion, so Judeo-Christian history—including mysticism—exists in a worldwide religious context. All the great religions have their mystics, who claim a direct encounter with the Infinite. Mystics in the differing great religions may disagree about the nature of the Deity; yet they seem to follow a path that has certain commonalities. Perhaps it is for this reason that many believers are wary of mysticism: it crops up everywhere, is hard to define or control, and suggests a religious unity where everyone else sees doctrinal diversity.

English thinker, Evelyn Underhill (1875–1941), calls mysticism the "art of union with Reality." She says the mystic is one who has attained that union to some degree, or who believes in such a union.[12] Herself a Christian and a major authority on mysticism, Underhill is inclined to think that mystics worldwide, in many faiths, are in touch with the same God and following a common mystical path. Other scholars hold that the experience of mystics in all the world's great religions is culturally conditioned. Mystics, according to this view, find the God they *expect* to find, the God of their prior religious and cultural conditioning, a God who differs more from that of other religions than might at first appear.[13] In certain other traditions, mystics, who have no belief in God, may find instead an intense experience of the sacred: enlightenment, *satori,* bliss.

MYSTICISM: MY VIEW AND APPROACH

Mysticism, in my view, is a deep and sustained intimacy with a loving God, sometimes marked and dramatic in its emotionality, more often anonymous and invisible to the casual observer. I agree with Thomas Corbishley about the bewildering and varied definitions of, and opinions about, this phenomenon. Such variations must be sorted out to gain a clear picture of the mystical life. My hope is to offer a simple entrance point into this vast territory.

definition

No attempt is made here to provide an exhaustive account of mysticism. Instead, I invite the reader to a thematic description, exploring some distinctive features of the mystical life: highs and lows, revelations and mysteries, biblical references and contemporary possibilities. The traditional language and approach of mysticism are evoked in time-honored terms: awakening, purgation, illumination, and union. I also offer my own vocabulary for the inner life: *beginning, yielding, darkness, transparency, fear of heights, hoops of steel,* and *clinging.* These terms are not exclusively mine, but they offer my perspective on life with God.

As these chapters unfold I trust the reader will glimpse the attractions of mystical life; the richly inspiring language of the mystics; acquaintance with some unusual mystical effects; a sense of the mystic path; most important of all, perhaps, a grasp of how "the mystics" connect with other believers; and finally, a sense of every believer's potential for walking the mystic path.

CHAPTER TWO

Who Can Be A Mystic?

t is difficult to draw a sharp line between those who are mystics and those who are merely far advanced in the spiritual life. No doubt many who are far advanced in the spiritual life would still modestly call themselves "beginners."

No doubt all—or most—of the canonized Christian saints are mystics, though their identity as mystics has not been proclaimed. Nor does the Roman Catholic Church look upon mysticism as a qualifying factor for sainthood. Saints are judged by the holiness of their lives, their sacrificial love for others; their presence in heaven is presumed from miracles attributed to their intercession after their deaths, as attested to by the living. In a sense, it seems that the official Church takes little or no account of mysticism. Saintliness, or holiness, is the deciding factor.

I see this in the light of grace. God takes the initiative, calling each one of us into a special and unique friendship. Each of us responds in a very personal way, more enthusiastically at certain times, hampered now and then by personal difficulties and doubts. Some never seem to hear God's call, or if they do, they refuse it. But those who do hear, respond in one way or another. Gradually, and in a mostly hidden manner, grace exerts its transforming influence.

Grace is offered. And yet the choosing is up to us. Each choice we make, C. S. Lewis says, brings us closer to heaven or drives us in the opposite direction. In *Mere Christianity* Lewis says:

> Every time you make a choice you are turning the central part of you, the part that chooses, into something a little different from what it was before. And taking your life as a whole, with all your innumerable choices, all your lifelong you are slowly turning this central thing into a creature that is in harmony with God, and with other creatures, and with itself, or else into one that is in a state of war. . . . Each of us at each moment is progressing to the one state or the other.[1]

Some decades ago, when I began to make a serious commitment to spiritual discipline, I began to observe how many others in the vast metropolis of New York City were doing so as well. My next door neighbor in our Queens neighborhood, a devout Jew, went to his law office in Manhattan by subway. On his walk to the train station (and on his rides to and from Manhattan) he listened to Torah tapes. He was practicing the discipline of study with every available moment. I myself never traveled without a small Bible thrust into the pocket of my raincoat, ready to be retrieved for prayer and reflection at a moment's notice. In the subway cars I saw people from many traditions at prayer. In the retreat houses of Long Island (and many other areas near New York) I discovered how many men and women were in serious pursuit of the life of the Spirit.

One of the first books I used when attempting an organized spiritual life was Evelyn Underhill's small volume, *Practical Mysticism*. Underhill seems to take it for granted that everyone is called to a kind of mystical life. But she also seems convinced that the vast majority of people do not hear this call, or fail to respond. In the opening passages of *Practical Mysticism* Underhill seems to be reporting the idle chatter of London dinner parties at which skeptics have asked her "What is mysticism?" without stopping to wait for an answer.

She reports on this as follows: "Those who are interested in that special attitude towards the universe which is now loosely called 'mystical' (this would of course be Underhill herself), find themselves beset by a multitude of persons who are constantly asking—some with real fervour, some with curiosity, and some with disdain—'What is mysticism?'" But when she answers their questions by suggesting they read the works of the mystics for themselves, they insist it is all too hard. "When referred to the writings of the mystics themselves, and to other works in which this question appears to be answered, these people reply that such books are wholly incomprehensible to them."

Underhill suspects that many of these inquiries may be less than sincere. Yet her heart goes out to the "genuine inquirer" who must contend with "self-appointed apostles who are eager to answer his question in many strange and inconsistent ways." These dinner party authorities will insist that mysticism is "a philosophy, an illusion, a kind of religion, a disease; that it means having visions, performing conjuring tricks, leading an idle, dreamy, and selfish life, neglecting one's business, wallowing in vague spiritual emotions, and being 'in tune with the infinite.'"

Underhill's witty strategy is first to make fun of all the irresponsible and foolish definitions of mysticism, and then to invite her "practical" reader to what she insists is the one satisfactory course: to find out the answer for herself or himself. Next, to encourage the practical man or woman, she offers her famous definition:

"Mysticism is the art of union with Reality. The mystic is a person who has attained that union in greater or less degree; or who aims at and believes in such attainment."

Immediately she admits that this answer is not very comforting. Another question immediately arises, "What is Reality?" And this is a question that may cause "infinite distress." Because only a mystic can answer it! And in terms which only "other mystics will understand."

It seems that Underhill, like many eager religious teachers, wants to shake us out of our lethargy; to kindle in us a desire for a higher and deeper life: "We know a thing only by uniting with it; by assimilating it; by an interpenetration of it and ourselves. It gives itself to us, just in so far as we give ourselves to it; and it is because our outflow towards things is always so perfunctory and so languid, that our comprehension of things is so perfunctory and languid too.[2] Underhill's definition of a mystic is broad enough to include both Walt Whitman and Teresa of Avila, the Sufi masters, and the Jewish mystical tradition. She comes to the heart of the question when she speaks of "the contemplative consciousness and claims it is "a faculty which is proper to all men, though few take the trouble to develop it." Those who do develop in the contemplative life gain entrance to a larger world: "Their attention to life has changed its character, sharpened its focus: and as a result they see, some a wider landscape, some a more brilliant, more significant, more detailed world than that which is apparent to the less educated, less observant vision of common sense."[3]

Would everyone agree that the contemplative consciousness is common to all? Would everyone agree that the mystical life and the contemplative life are one and the same? Probably not.

16

In fact, it would be hard to suppose that "everyone" could agree on matters related to mysticism, as it is the business of scholars (and the world in general) to disagree.

Who, then, can be a mystic? And what is the point of even raising the question?

WHO WOULD CHOOSE THE ECSTATIC LIFE?

In recent years two novels have been written about women visionaries, both of them, to my mind at least, seemingly drawn from the experiences of Therese of Lisieux.

One is entitled *Mariette in Ecstasy,* by Ron Hansen.[4] It takes place in a convent in upstate New York in the early twentieth century, where a cloistered woman has visions of God. Her experiences cause great jealousies and dissensions in her religious community. Ultimately she must leave the convent, and her visions disappear.

The second is entitled *Lying Awake,* by Mark Salzman.[5] Set in a Carmelite monastery outside present-day Los Angeles in the late 1960s, it concerns Sister John of the Cross who is known within her community for religious visions, ecstasies, and the writings in which she describes them. But when Sister John begins to have severe headaches, she learns that a brain disorder—epilepsy—may be the reason for it all. Should she consent to an operation, which will relieve the symptoms, but may deprive her of visions as well?

Both of these novels are excellent contemporary treatments of one aspect of the mystical life: a life of ecstasies, visions and apparitions. No doubt the reason that most of us are wary of mysticism is that our definition of mystic has something to do with bizarre, far out aspects of experience. Interestingly, in both novels the central character, the mystic, returns from the high reaches of mystical experience to a more earthbound life.

If mysticism were only about ecstasies, who would want to be a mystic? Does anyone really want a life of spiritual thrill-seeking? Are we itching to walk the farthest boundaries of experience?

WHY ARE PEOPLE WARY?

In the Western tradition, the mystical life is focused upon union or intimacy with God.

In 2001, I wrote to my lifelong friend John Williams via e-mail. He had long been interested in mysticism and was well read on the subject. Our correspondence was by international e-mail: he in his home outside London and I in Louisiana. I told him that many of my acquaintances are wary of the word "mysticism," preferring to speak of "contemplation" instead.

His reply, entitled "Mysticism and . . ." dated October 7, 2001, was sharp:

> About mysticism: why are people wary of the word? Too strong? It is what it is. Contemplation is usually a part of being a mystic but I was taught while studying the Spanish mystics (St. Teresa de Avila, St. John of the Cross, possibly Fray Luis de Leon) that to truly become one with God (the aim of the true mystic) a lot more is needed. The second edition of the New Shorter Oxford English Dictionary defines mysticism as "the beliefs or mental tendencies characteristic of mystics; belief in the possibility of union with or absorption into God by means of contemplation and self-surrender; belief in or reliance on the possibility of spiritual apprehension of knowledge inaccessible to the intellect." I remember that a lot of commentators and writers I read thought that a true mystic fits into a certain physical/mental/psychological/spiritual profile. Not everyone can become one. The Sufi Dervishes use those whirling dances as one of their ways of going beyond this world. Buddhists sublimate and eventually eliminate their personality in search of Nirvana. And so on . . .

Sorry to rabbit on, but I just don't think you can equate contemplation and mysticism. They are steps on the same journey, but millions more can contemplate, or learn how to, than can become a true mystic. That is something that cannot be learnt.

Though my friend John Williams was no theologian, he had struck on precisely the point that fits perfectly with a theologically Christian view of mysticism. This state of intimate communion with God is a gift of grace.

The mystics do not desire to become mystics. They desire to know God at the greatest level of intimacy possible for themselves. And they know their limitations. They see themselves as flawed and sinful human beings, in need of God's redeeming grace. They come as beggars to the throne, not saying, "Lord, please make me a mystic," but rather, "Lord, I want to know you better."

I would agree, then, with John Williams, as with many other commentators on mysticism, that contemplation is not mysticism, but a step along the way.

At the same time, those who are called to prayer—to contemplative prayer—and perhaps ultimately to mystical prayer, are people who must choose to accept the gift. But a certain logic must prevail here. People who become mystics are people who have opened themselves up to the practice of the spiritual life. What practice or practices does that entail?

A CAUTIONARY LETTER

In "Christian Meditation: a Letter to the Bishops of the Catholic Church on Some Aspects of Christian Meditation," the Congregation for the Doctrine of the Faith[6] issued some cautions for Christians who had become entranced by Eastern forms of meditation. "The love of God, the sole object of Christian contemplation, is a reality which cannot be 'mastered' by any method or technique. On the contrary, we must always have our sights fixed on Jesus Christ, in whom God's love went to the cross for us and there he assumed even the condition of estrangement from the Father (cf. Mk. 15:34). We therefore should allow God to decide the ways he wishes to have us participate in his love."

The letter on Christian meditation is careful to state that the majority of great religions have sought union with God and also have suggested ways to go about arriving at such a union. Repeating language from the Vatican Council document, *Nostra Aetate*, the letter asserts: "Just as 'the Catholic Church rejects nothing of what is true and holy in these religions,' neither should these ways be rejected out of hand simply because they are not Christian." At the same time the letter voices a concern about experimentation on the part of Christians whose spiritual lives are not well formed.

From the earliest times, these church fathers seem to be saying, the church has advised the practice of *sentire cum ecclesia*, that is, thinking with the church. Spiritual masters or guides, following this practice, warn and caution their pupils against inappropriate teachings and practices; at the same time, the spiritual master leads his or her pupil into the life of prayer by example, heart to heart, seeking always the guidance of the Holy Spirit.

What, then, of mystical graces? Possibly the founder of a particular religious group or society has received such extraordinary graces. But that doesn't mean that the members and disciples of her congregation will all receive, or should aspire to the same graces. Mystical gifts are particular and personal.

"With regard to mysticism, one has to distinguish between the gifts of the Holy Spirit and the charisms granted by God in a totally gratuitous way. The former are something which every Christian can quicken in himself by his zeal for the life of faith, hope and charity." The document refers us once again to the cautions offered by the Apostle Paul in his first letter to the Corinthians (1 Cor. 14:6–12). It also points out that the gifts of the spirit are not the same as extraordinary mystical graces—here the text to be consulted is Paul's Letter to the Romans (Rom. 12:3–21).

PORTRAIT OF A MODERN MYSTIC

What is the relationship between mystical life and holiness? Mystical life—in my definition of close intimacy with a loving God—will surely manifest itself in holiness.[7] No doubt the ideal picture of a mystic has already been voiced by Jesus of Nazareth in his sermon on the mount. Such a radically virtuous and holy person is pure in heart, peace loving, a peacemaker, poor in spirit, willing to be persecuted for righteousness' sake, loving to God and neighbor. This is the compassionate person, who, when asked for his shirt, offers his cloak also. When asked to go a short distance, he or she goes a longer one. He or she is childlike, for of such is the kingdom of heaven.[8]

Do we have such people among us? We do. And many of them go unrecognized. I would mention one of my own mystic candidates for the kingdom of heaven described by Jesus.

Simone Weil (1909–1943) was a French social activist and political radical who is now thought to be a remarkable twentieth-century mystic. Born a Jew, the daughter of a middle class Parisian doctor, she was sensitized to political issues by World War I, and involved in a variety of pro-worker movements throughout the 1930s.

Weil was not always sweet-tempered, and certainly she was not mild, at least in her days of studying philosophy at the Sorbonne, when she crossed daggers with Simone de Beauvoir in conversation. Beauvoir was saying that what people needed most was meaning in their lives. Eric O. Springsted relates how the incident unfolded: "Weil frostily replied, quickly looking her over, that it was clear she had not ever gone hungry, a remark that Beauvoir recognized as putting her and her philosophy in its place as belonging to the petty bourgeoisie." But Beauvoir remembered Weil, not for her dagger-like wit, but for her compassion. Simone Weil once melted into tears when she heard of the widespread death and destruction caused by an earthquake in China.

Feeling a deep solidarity with the ordinary worker, the young middle class Frenchwoman spent a year working in three factories in Paris. Afterwards she wrote an essay, "Reflections Concerning the Causes of Liberty and Social Oppression." It was a critique of Marx and an attempt to understand the dignity of the worker.

In her autobiography Weil mentioned three contacts with Christianity that made a difference in her life. The first was in Portugal, when she witnessed a religious procession going through the streets. Reflecting on the experience, she saw suddenly that Christianity was "the religion of slaves" and that she was one of its slaves as well. In 1937, while visiting Assisi, she "felt compelled to go down on her knees." In 1938 she and her mother made a visit to the Abbey at Solesmes at Holy Week. There she reported that Christ took hold of her. A young Catholic she met during that week introduced her to the poetry of George Herbert. She memorized his poem, "Love," and recited it to herself frequently, especially when afflicted with a migraine headache. "It was during one of those recitations that . . . Christ himself came down and took possession of me." From then on she believed in the love of Jesus and in his divinity; she was strongly moved by the meaning of the Passion.

Many have been moved by Herbert's poem:

> Love bade me welcome; yet my soul drew back
> Guilty of dust and sin.
> But quick-eyed Love, observing me grow slack

From my first entrance in,
Drew nearer to me, sweetly questioning
If I lacked anything.

A guest, I answered, worthy to be here.
Love said, You shall be he.
I, the unkind, the ungrateful? Ah my dear,
I cannot look on thee.
Love took my hand, and smiling did reply,
Who made the eyes but I?

Truth, Lord, but I have marred them; let my shame
Go where it doth deserve.
And know you not, says Love, who bore the blame?
My dear, then I will serve.
You must sit down, says Love, and taste my meat.
Then I did sit and eat.

Driven by the anti-Semitic persecutions of that era, Weil went to Provence, where she worked as an agricultural laborer on Gustave Thibon's farm; there she discovered the relationship between prayer, God, and Eucharist, but hesitated to become a formal Christian because of her solidarity with persecuted Judaism. She relates in her autobiography the mystical encounter with Christ which developed while she was working on Thibon's farm. There she adopted the practice of reciting the Our Father very attentively in Greek. "With absolute attention," is Weil's phrase. This had a remarkable effect: "The infinity of the ordinary expanses of perception is replaced by an infinity to the second or sometimes the third degree. At the same time, filling every part of this infinity of infinity, there is silence, a silence which is not the absence of sound but which is the object of a positive sensation, more positive than that of sound."

And Weil went further: "Sometimes during this recitation or at other moments, Christ is really present with me in person."

But if you had actually met Simone Weil, would you have liked her? Her pride, her sharp tongue, her ambition, her desire to be great—including a far-fetched scheme she presented to Charles DeGaulle for women nurses to be dropped by parachute at the battlefront in World War II—all these indicate her highly melodramatic personality, her eccentricity. Would you have thought her a mystic, a model for Christian spirituality, or merely a *poseur*? Personally, I find much to like about her. Especially, I identify with Weil's attraction to the African American churches in Harlem, New York City. Weil, during her time in New York City, visited these churches because she loved the joyfulness, the inner freedom, the celebration.

Educated in philosophy and experienced as a schoolteacher, Weil did not hesitate to comment on her experience of Jesus Christ. She wrote many essays on prayer, fidelity to Christ, and contemplative experience. In particular she developed a theological interpretation of suffering and affliction. *Waiting for God* is her best-known work.

Weil engaged in the practice of fasting in ways that were probably immoderate. During the early part of the war she tried to restrict her intake of food to what the French in occupied France were getting. This may have precipitated her collapse from tuberculosis; she knew she had contracted TB but fasted anyhow. She died in England (Ashford, Kent) in August, 1943.[9]

Whatever the quirks of her personality, Weil is now recognized as a mystic and an insightful commentator on the spiritual life. Her life was short, but her influence has been pervasive. The love of God and of others consumed her. Her profound poetic spirit has moved many others to a deeper consideration of the meaning of God's love.

THE ANONYMOUS MYSTIC

I believe that we are meeting mystics every day, but we do not recognize them. Their humility and modesty is such that they pass into the crowd ("So they picked up stones to throw at him; but Jesus hid himself and went out of the temple" Jn. 8:59). Perhaps we could spot them by their spiritual disciplines: prayer, meditation, fasting, study, simplicity, solitude, submission, service, confession, worship, guidance, and celebration.[10] It is possible, but not likely. For real mystics practice their deep love and service to God in ways that may fly below the radar, unobtrusively, transforming the lives of others in ways that seem sublimely plain spoken and level-headed. Except when they receive extraordinary mystical gifts (not everyone does) it is hard to pick them out in a crowd. We have noted earlier that Padre Pio looked much like the next monk in the procession. More to the point, the Roman soldiers needed Judas to point Jesus out to them. To them, he looked more or less like any other Galilean.

Both Thomas Merton and Karl Rahner, a major modern Catholic theologian, insist on a mysticism of ordinary living. For Merton, the incarnation has sanctified all of human living. Far from taking the contemplative above and beyond the ordinary, contemplation, if it is authentic, roots the human being in the ordinary. The ordinary routine of daily life becomes the texture of contemplation for the devoted Christian. Merton insists there is a "latent, or implicit, infused dimension to all prayer." Thus Merton gives us a valuable insight into the possibility of an ordinary or a hidden mysticism. He calls it "masked contemplation."

Perhaps, as we shall see, this "masked contemplation" is what John Wesley saw as "a mysticism of service."[11] Thomas Merton sees the hidden or "masked" contemplative as one who finds God in active service to the poor, the despised, the people at the margins of life. These "masked contemplatives" do not have the luxury to spend long hours in silence and solitude. But their mystic encounter with Jesus comes in service to the littlest and the least. They are mystics, perhaps, without knowing it, for they are fully in touch with the heart of God. Nevertheless, their mysticism is authentic.[12]

In different language Karl Rahner makes a similar claim: everyone is called to the immediacy of God's presence. A supernatural, graced, "anonymously Christian" mysticism may even exist outside of Christianity; that is to say, Christ himself may be working outside of established Christianity to be in touch with mystics (known and unknown) in all parts of the globe. Rahner sets no limits on the power of God.

Rahner writes: "In every human being . . . there is something like an anonymous, unthematic, perhaps repressed, basic experience of being orientated to God, which is constitutive of man in his concrete make-up (of nature and grace), which can be repressed but not destroyed, which is 'mystical' or (if you prefer a more cautious terminology) has its climax in what the older teachers called infused contemplation."[13]

This is no claim of universalism. Rahner says that God is everywhere at work, and everywhere takes the divine initiative. He does not say that all human beings equally recognize and respond to that call. But Rahner does not envision a mysticism of interiority alone. Instead, he sees a mystical dimension in many aspects of living, a mysticism of eating, drinking, sleeping, walking, sitting, and other everyday experience. Even more than these, Rahner sees Christ coming to meet us in our loneliness, our rejections, our unrequited loves, our faith in the face of death.

Even so, in the strands of thought and reflection taken here from these two modern thinkers and mystics is the beginning of a full theology of the mystical; one that can undergird my own sense that God's call is to each of us. Human responses will vary. To become a mystic is not (for most) to become an ecstatic in some melodramatic style; but rather to enter into a deep encounter with God in a humble, hidden, and entirely mysterious way. It is about God's unfailing love. It is about the mystery of the cross. It is about an encounter with the power of God in the middle of things: an encounter that is hidden, inexpressible, ineffable, and real.

WHO CAN BE A MYSTIC?

The term "mystic," like the term "saint," is best conferred on a person by the judgment of others, and after a considerable lapse of time. Opinion is divided as to whether mysticism is related to temperamental factors or is possible for all human beings. Yet it is evident that mystics are modest folk whose concentration is on God, not upon themselves. To appropriate the title of "mystic" is not in keeping with the mystical path. But God is no respecter of persons, and may call the most unlikely of us to intimate knowledge of divine love.

LEARNING FROM THE MYSTICS

In the following pages we will sample many aspects of the mystic path: the sense of dwelling in God or in Christ that is the major theme of Paul the Apostle; the profound influence of nature upon some mystics; such common metaphors for the mystic life as "path," "journey," and "way." Group Mysticism will be examined. A mysticism of everyday life will be explored. In no sense is this a how-to book for becoming a mystic. At the same time, plunging into the mystic life does open us up to the depth and power of God's grace. Some definite clues may be found to encourage the life of the Spirit.

CHAPTER THREE

The Mysticism of Paul

s we have already seen, mysticism has deep
biblical roots. Perhaps the most notable
Christian mystic in history is the Apostle
Paul. Yet mysticism is only one of his gifts.
In fact, because Paul the Apostle is such a
major theological figure in Christianity,
we sometimes forget to place him among
the mystics.[1] The popular image of Paul is one of active
apostolic zeal. He is depicted on the road, on the sea, taking
risks for the spreading of Christian faith throughout the
ancient world, arguing, speaking, persuading. He does not fit
the stereotype of mystic—a solitary person of contemplative
prayer. Yet Paul's writing is shot through with references to
prayer, to the influence of Spirit, divine providence, an
indwelling fire that makes itself known in a thousand ways.

Much of Christian belief and teaching rests on Paul's mystical formulations.

"Christian mysticism has its roots in pre-Christian history," Evelyn Underhill writes. She suggests that Saul of Tarsus (whose Roman name was Paul) was steeped in the Hebrew Scriptures, especially the prophetic writings, and "accepting without question the prophetic claim to a firsthand experience of God."[2] In early Hebrew prophetic religion, Underhill says, ecstasy was cultivated and courted by music and dancing as well as prayer. The Hebrew prophet laid himself open to being possessed by the Divine. The prophetic ideal is a mystical ideal: the reluctant Jeremiah accepting God's commands, or Isaiah going barefoot for three years, dressed as a captive, in obedience to God. In short, we may imagine Paul/Saul as a man with a mystical bent and a deep affinity for God even before his personal encounter with the risen Jesus on the Damascus Road.

Saul/Paul was a Pharisee, a student of the eminent teacher Gamaliel. The Pharisees were one of several sects that dominated Second-Temple Judaism. Soon after the destruction of the temple, the title of Pharisee disappeared, because most Jews had become Pharisees. Yet in the New Testament, Pharisee connotes not devotion, but hypocrisy and narrow-mindedness. In fact the Pharisees and the followers of Jesus held much in common: belief in an afterlife in which good and evil deeds would be judged and rewarded (which the Sadducees did not accept); belief in a Messiah who would usher in a time of universal peace and bring Jews back from the four corners of the earth to Israel. Great teachers of Talmudic Judaism, such as Hillel, Rabbi Yochanan ben Zakkai, and Rabbi Akiva were Pharisees.[3]

Christians may be deeply suspicious of the Judaism of Paul/Saul because he enters the Christian story as the one who held the cloaks of those who stoned Stephen. But in fact, to be a Pharisee (in Paul's time and later) was to be a devout follower of God. Jewish Pharisaic beliefs would have molded Paul: the doctrine of providence, the divine ordering of the world, reward and punishment beyond the grave, the resurrection of the dead, the Ten Commandments, love of God and neighbor, belief in angels and devils. Scholars can trace the influence of the rabbis upon his speech and thought. When he quotes Scripture, it is the Septuagint (Greek translation of the Hebrew Bible) that he cites. One is inclined to think that Paul became a mystic because of his encounter with the risen Jesus. But was he not already prepared, by his experience as a Pharisee, to have a close and intimate relationship to God? In recent times some scholars have suggested that Jesus himself, while not a Pharisee, was formed by an equally intense school of devotion and prayer. It could be said that the first-century denomination, or sect, of the Pharisees was a school of mysticism, a school of passionate devotion to God.

A MYSTICAL CONVERSION

Paul's first great claim to our attention is his remarkable vision on the Damascus road, and the amazing events that followed. As told in the Acts of the Apostles, the story of Paul's vision and conversion happens not only to Saul/Paul but to others in the community of Jesus' followers. When Saul's journey is interrupted by a blinding light the risen Jesus speaks to him. Saul loses his sight; he also receives guidance to go to a certain house where healing and acceptance by devout followers of Jesus await him.

> While I was on my way and approaching Damascus, about noon a great light from heaven suddenly shone about me. I fell to the ground and heard a voice saying to me, "Saul, Saul, why are you persecuting me?" I answered, "Who are you, Lord?" Then he said to me, "I am Jesus of Nazareth

whom you are persecuting." Now those who were with me saw the light but did not hear the voice of the one who was speaking to me. I asked, "What am I to do, Lord?" The Lord said to me, "Get up and go to Damascus. There you will be told everything that has been assigned to you to do." Since I could not see because of the brightness of the light, those who were with me took my hand and led me to Damascus (Acts 22:6–11).

Ananias also receives divine instruction to go to that same house, and finds Paul there. "A certain Ananias who was a devout man according to the law and well spoken of by all the Jews living there, came to me; and standing beside me, he said: 'Brother Saul, regain your sight.' In that very hour I regained my sight and saw him" (Acts 22:12-13). Ananias doesn't stop there. "Then he said, 'The God of our ancestors has chosen you to know his will, to see The Righteous One and hear his own voice, for you will be his witness to all the world of what you have seen and heard" (Acts 22:14-15). Ananias encourages him to accept Christ and be baptized.

Paul goes on to recount a further mystical contact. "After I had returned to Jerusalem and while I was praying in the temple, I fell into a trance and saw Jesus saying to me, 'Hurry and get out of Jerusalem quickly, because they will not accept your testimony about me" (Acts 22:17-18).

In both these encounters, the one on the Damascus Road and the one in the temple, Paul gives account of mystical, Spirit-filled experiences.

IN OR OUT OF THE BODY

Then there is Paul's account of his own apocalyptic rapture to the third heaven (2 Cor. 12:1–6): "I know a person in Christ who fourteen years ago was caught up to the third heaven— whether in the body or out of the body I do not know; God knows. And I know that such a person—whether in the body or out of the body I do not know; God knows—was caught up into Paradise and heard things that are not to be told, that no mortal is permitted to repeat."

Paul's account is considered remarkable among first-century apocalyptic writings because (in spite of the fact that he refers to himself in the third person, with seeming anonymity) it is a firsthand account. On this point scholars agree. Why is it rare? Most such stories in apocalyptic literature are pseudonymous, that is, ascribed to biblical writers whose names are famous, and who belong, by and large, to an earlier period. Paul's is unique.[4]

These visions are not the only reasons we may consider Paul to be a mystic. His discourse is filled with ways of speaking about God and Christ which are rare, special, inspired by an intimate knowledge of the Almighty.

One of Paul's most memorable statements about God is found in Acts 17:28: "For in him we live and move and have our being." This statement is not just a theological formula, it is a description of the encounter between God and humanity. It is an existential statement. Paul says we *exist* in God, we live and move in him. Throughout his letters Paul also speaks of being *in Christ,* or *in Christ Jesus.* Paul uses the phrase "in Christ" fifty times! Paul is describing an immediate encounter. God is not merely over us, ruling us, but we are actually embraced by him, we exist in him, within his being.

Paul makes many other statements about God and Christ. There is, for example, his observation in Romans 14:7–9: "We do not live to ourselves, and we do not die to ourselves. If we live, we live to the Lord, and if we die, we die to the Lord; so then, whether we live or whether we die, we are the Lord's. For to this end Christ died and lived again, that he might be Lord of both the dead and the living." So familiar are most Christians with this teaching that they may overlook its mystical power. It suggests that the veil between this life and the next has faded away in Christ. Paul finds himself living in two realms at once, the present life and the life beyond.

Sometimes it seems that Paul is using poetic language, that his speech is weighted with metaphor. Yet Paul's force and sincerity show that these metaphors are not "figures of speech" to him. They are his only ways to express realities he has seen through revelation.

For example, in Galatians 2:19–21 he writes: "I have been crucified with Christ; and it is no longer I who live, but it is Christ who lives in me. And the life I now live in the flesh I live by faith in the Son of God, who loved me and gave himself for me." This is mystical language, inspired by a personal encounter with God.

Throughout his letters to the churches Paul constantly describes a Christian community bound together by mystical love—God's love reflected in love of neighbor. Consider what Paul writes in his First Letter to the Thessalonians: "Be at peace among yourselves. And we urge you, beloved, to admonish the idlers, encourage the faint hearted, help the weak, be patient with all of them. . . . Rejoice always, pray without ceasing, give thanks in all circumstances, for this is the will of God in Christ Jesus for you. Do not quench the Spirit. Do not despise the words of the prophets, but test everything; hold fast to what is good; abstain from every form of evil" (1 Thess. 5:13–22). Paul is describing not a rigid adherence to codes of behavior, but a life transformed by love.

There has been much debate about what Paul describes as his "thorn in the flesh." Was it a besetting sin? A recurring illness? Even, perhaps, the stigmata or wounds of Christ, experienced by certain mystics later on in Christian history? There is really no way of knowing. Clearly, Paul has been transformed by his encounter with Christ. His "thorn in the flesh" does not discourage him. He continues to take extraordinary risks with his life, undergoing shipwrecks, persecutions, imprisonment, floggings, and finally (according to tradition) martyrdom.

More is directly known about Paul's personality and experience than about the other apostles. We even have a description of him gleaned from early literature: a short, bald man with a thick beard and a pronounced nose, his eyebrows meeting and his legs slightly bowed.[5] We also know enough about Paul to call him a mystic. In fact, the experience of dwelling in Christ, in the Spirit, in God, was probably common to all the early disciples, inspired as they were through post-resurrection appearances, the descent of the Holy Spirit at Pentecost, remarkable healings, unusual escapes from prison, angelic appearances. But mysticism is not simply a matter of rare and unusual phenomena. Remarkable religious expressions may happen when hearts are on fire for God, but mysticism should not be equated with the strange or the paranormal. Paul himself, in his First Letter to the Corinthians admits that he himself has the gift of tongues, but he insists that believers should not covet such gifts or be vain about having them. A thoroughgoing detachment about spiritual gifts is the proper, level-headed and faithful Christian way. "Now concerning spiritual gifts, brothers and sisters, I do not want you to be uninformed. . . . Now there are varieties of gifts, but the same Spirit. . . . But strive for the greater gifts. And I will show you a still more excellent way" (1 Cor. 12:1, 4, 31).

WHAT IS PAUL'S "EXCELLENT WAY"?

The more excellent way that Paul describes in 1 Corinthians 13 is love. "If I speak in the tongues of mortals and of angels, and have not love, I am a noisy gong or a clanging cymbal." Giving away one's possessions, having prophetic powers, being able to work miracles, Paul discounts all this as having no meaning without love. The love Paul speaks of is unselfish, kind, never possessive, always generous. Paul is contrasting narrow, competitive human love, with *agape*, the most godly love. Such love, as we shall see, is at the center of the mystical encounter. The mystic experiences God as love, a love of such depth and power and mystery that it cannot be fully explained and described, except (and then only imperfectly) in the language of poetry and metaphor. It is the love God expresses to us in Jeremiah 31:3: "I have loved you with an everlasting love." It is the passionate love described in the Song of Solomon (3:4): "I found him whom my soul loves/I held him and would not let him go." Or again, "I am my beloved's and he is mine" (Song 6:3). Mysticism should never be limited to ecstatic phenomena, never marked by thrill-seeking. Mysticism is rooted in love: love that sometimes overflows in a current of joy.

CHAPTER FOUR

Earth's Crammed with Heaven

 hildren and adults of a certain sensitivity report a sense of sacredness in particular moments under the influence of nature's wonders. In the words of the psalmist:

The heavens are telling the glory of God;
    and the firmament proclaims his handiwork.
Day to day pours forth speech,
and night to night declares knowledge.

(Ps. 19:1-2)

For some, the first authentic experience of God, the first sense of really knowing God, comes in an encounter with the beauty of the natural world.

Christian mystical writers such as Gerard Manley Hopkins, while holding an orthodox theology, sense the presence of God in nature. In the writings of C. S. Lewis, Thomas Merton and Bede Griffiths we find hints of nature mysticism: the sense of awe beside a flowering currant bush, Merton's childhood experience of "the birds are in church," and Bede Griffiths wanting to fall on his knees, convinced he was in the divine presence among natural things.

> One day during my last term at school I walked out alone in the evening and heard the birds singing in that full chorus of song which can only be heard at that time of the year at dawn or sunset," Bede Griffiths (1906–1994) wrote in his conversion story, *The Golden String*. "I remember now," he continued, "the shock of surprise with which the sound broke on my ears. It seemed to me that I had never heard the birds singing before and I wondered whether they sang like this all year long and I had never noticed it. As I walked on I came to some hawthorn trees in full bloom and again I thought that I had never seen such a sight nor experienced such sweetness before. If I had been brought suddenly among the trees of the Garden of Paradise and heard a choir of angels singing I could not have been more surprised.

Griffith's story begins with a loving response to some unseen, hidden presence among natural things.

> I came then to where the sun was setting over the playing fields. A lark rose suddenly from the ground beside the tree where I was standing and poured out its song above my head, and then sank still singing to rest. Everything then grew still as the sunset faded and the veil of dusk began to cover the earth. I remember now the feeling of awe which came over me. I felt inclined to kneel on the ground, as though I had been standing in the presence of an angel; and I hardly dared to look on the face of the sky, because it seemed as though it was but a veil before the face of God.[1]

What Griffiths felt was more than just a response to flowers, trees, dusk, birdsong; the beauty of the natural world. Instead he was describing a sense of religious awe; he found himself grasping a hidden dimension to the world, something beyond the world of sense, something greater and higher. At first this experience seemed to draw him away from Christianity as he knew it; but soon he saw he was being called to experience the Christian God more fully. Ultimately Griffiths, influenced by the nature poets like William Wordsworth, who stopped short of Christian belief, fully embraced Christian faith. He became a man of intense and passionate prayer.

Evelyn Underhill, in her discussion of the illumination of the self, interprets such an impulse well:

> We have seen that all real artists, as well as all pure mystics, are sharers to some degree in the Illuminated Life. They have drunk, with [William] Blake, from that cup of intellectual vision which is the chalice of the Spirit of Life: know something of its divine inebriation whenever Beauty inspires them to create. Some have only sipped it. . . . but to all who have seen Beauty face to face, the Grail has been administered; and through that sacramental communion they are made participants in the mystery of the world.[2]

A COMMON FORM OF RELIGIOUS ILLUMINATION

Underhill says that seeing God in nature, and so attaining "a radiant consciousness of the 'otherness' of natural things," is one of the commonest form of religious illumination. This apprehension of God may be only partial, but it leads to still further illuminations, until, as with William Blake, "we reach the point at which the mystic swallows up the poet." William Blake (1757-1827) was a Christian poet and visual artist who was possessed by religious and spiritual illumination. It was not only nature that set him on fire. He was also alight with the heavenly vision, as revealed in sacred Scripture. His mystical grasp of God's presence in the world of created things was a vision he struggled to express:

> To see a World in a Grain of Sand,
>   And a Heaven in a Wild Flower
> Hold Infinity in the palm of your hand
> And Eternity in an hour[3]

Many poets write about the beauties of nature. But few are identified as mystics. "Blake conceived that it was his vocation to bring this mystical illumination, this heightened vision of reality, within the range of ordinary men; to 'cleanse the doors of perception' of the race," Underhill explains. "'Dear Sir, excuse my enthusiasm, or rather madness,' Blake, who was also a graphic artist, wrote in one of his letters, 'for I am really drunk with intellectual vision whenever I take a pencil or graver into my hand.'"[4] Blake's vision is mystical in that he sees beyond the beauty of any particular thing to the vision of God. When poets do this, if we do not call them mystics, at least we may call them mystical.

The American poet Emily Dickinson (1830–1886) is a keen observer of nature. She praises its beauties. In and through them she sees the wonder of God. Her Christianity has been questioned as to its orthodoxy. (This could be said of the Puritan John Milton as well.) But a larger understanding of her poetic vision places her among the mystical writers.

> I never saw a Moor—
>   I never saw the Sea—
> Yet I know how the Heather looks
>   And what a Billow be.
>
> I never spoke with God
>   Nor visited in Heaven
> Yet certain am I of the spot
>   As if the Checks were given—[5]

CHRIST PRESENT IN ALL THINGS

One of the most celebrated of Christian mystical, nature poets is Gerard Manley Hopkins, (1844–1889) who sees God present in all created things.

> The world is charged with the grandeur of God;
> It will flame out, like shining from shook foil;
> It gathers to a greatness. . . .[6]

An early hint of Hopkins' sensitivity to nature and God may be found in his account of a day spent boating on the river during his Oxford undergraduate days:

> Yesterday afternoon, Strachan-Davidson and I went boating on the upper river. We took a sailing boat, skulled up and sailed down. We then took canoes. I know nothing so luxuriously delicious as a canoe. It is a long light-covered boat, the same shape both ways, with an opening in the middle where you recline, your feet against one board, your back against a cushion on another. You look, contrary of course to ordinary boats, in the direction in which you are going, and move with a single paddle—a rod with a broad round blade at either end which you dip alternately on either side. The motion is Elysian. Strachan-Davidson's canoe being very low in the water and the wind being very high and making waves, he shipped much water, till he said that it was more pleasant than safe, and had to get to shore and bale out the water, which had nearly sunk him. I, rejoicing in the security of a boat high in the water and given me because large and safe, was meanwhile washed onto the opposite lee shore where I was comfortable but embarrassed, and could not get off it for some time. Altogether it was Paradisaical. A canoe in the Cherwell must be the summit of human happiness.

Hopkins uses the same comparison to Paradise that Griffiths would later employ.[7]

For Hopkins a youthful love of nature was only a beginning point for mysticism, which came into full focus after he chose the discipline of Roman Catholicism and the constraints of a Jesuit religious vocation: Hopkins exhibited a passionate willingness to take chances with life. He risked everything for God. His commitment to Jesus Christ in the Roman Catholic Church cost him a great deal; but that was only the beginning of his tremendous gamble. This risking everything for God led to a willingness to embrace Jesuit obedience, however it tethered and constrained him; yet that, it seems is what set Hopkins free for an almost childlike gamboling on the hillsides. The restrictiveness of the Jesuit life, together with the mystical intensity of his rule-bound spirituality, in combination gave rise to a special kind of focus. Hopkins was able to structure the whole of creation into world-embracing metaphors: crystalline images that reveal cosmic realities.

> As kingfishers catch fire, dragonflies draw flame;
> As tumbled over rim in roundy wells
> Stones ring; like each tucked string tells, each hung bell's
> Bow swung finds tongue to fling out broad its name;
> Each mortal thing does one thing and the same;
> Deals out that being indoors each one dwells;
> Selves—goes itself; myself it speaks and spells,
> Crying What I do is me; for that I came.[8]

Nature Poets: A Long Tradition

Hopkins is part of a long tradition of British nature poets who exhibit a religious intensity. Evelyn Underhill mentions several of these, almost in a glancing way: Tennyson's "Flower in the Crannied Wall," Vaughan's "Each bush and oak doth know I AM." They are examples of what she terms "the simple vision of pure love."[9] To these might readily be added Elizabeth Barrett Browning's lines,

> Earth's crammed with heaven,
> And every common bush afire with God.
> But only he who sees takes off his shoes—
> The rest sit round it and pluck blackberries.[10]

and Christina Rossetti's:

> Spring bursts today
> For Christ is risen
> and all the earth's at play.[11]

Hopkins was not only a poet, but also a theorist about poetry, developing ideas about the nature of poetry and of experience. One important influence on him was the Franciscan philosopher Duns Scotus (c.1266–1308) whose idea of "thisness" (*haecceitas*) struck a chord with Hopkins. Scotus, known as the Subtle Doctor, along with his school, held that reality—divine reality—could be glimpsed in and through the particular. This notion, "thisness" or *haecceitas* corresponds to a Jesuit insight made popular centuries later by Ignatius Loyola: for the prayerful person, God can be sought and found "in all things."

Thomas Merton is one of the most articulate voices of contemplation in modern life. In his book, *The Seven Storey Mountain*, he recalls the moment when, as a child, he saw a flock of birds fly up, and heard church bells, and said to his father, "Father, all the birds are in their church. Can we go too?"[12]

But Merton never fully outgrew this childhood vision of God glimpsed through nature. In his journals and diaries, he gives a continuing account of his experience of God, as it were, in the wild.[13] His love of solitude was pronounced, and with it came a continuing passion for the natural world. Merton had been originally attracted to the Franciscans because of their reputed love of God's creation. He feared that as a Cistercian he might be cut off from nature and its hidden wonders. But

43

Merton had misread the Cistercians: in fact, Merton's superiors encouraged him to follow his call to silence and solitude. At the rural Gethsemani monastery in Kentucky, he gained permission to spend time meditating in the woods, which gave him great contentment and joy. Merton recorded many details of this: "Right under me was a dry creek, with clean pools lying like glass between the shale pavement of the stream, and the shale was as white and crumpled as sea-biscuit." In the same passage he captures his response to the birds: "Down in the glen were songs of marvelous birds. I saw the gold-orange flame of an oriole in a tree. Orioles are too shy to come near the monastery. There was a cardinal whistling somewhere, but the best song was that of two birds that sounded as wonderfully as nightingales and their song echoed through the wood. I had never heard such birds before. The echo made the place sound more remote and self-contained, more perfectly enclosed, and more like Eden."[14] Eden again! The Eden reference here is one small example of Merton's tendency to read the book of nature in the light of Scripture and revelation. He found moral and spiritual lessons in the natural world. It is reminiscent of Shakespeare's line, about finding "sermons in stones/and good in everything."[15]

More importantly, Merton saw this connection to the natural world as essential to contemplative life, a proper antidote to the influences of technological society. It was all about healing "the post-Cartesian technologism that separates man from the world."[16] In *Search for Solitude* he wrote: "I want not only to observe but to know living things, and this implies a dimension of primordial familiarity which is simple and primitive and religious and poor."[17] Merton defines this as "connatural knowing," which is a "mode of apprehension" that "reaches out to grasp the inner reality, the vital substance of its object, by a kind of affective identification of itself with it."[18]

For Merton this integration with the natural world is an essential component of any authentic human life, but especially of a life that aspires to contemplation. The natural world is a source of revelation, a way to connect with the divine Ground of all created reality, which at the same time transcends created reality. "When your mind is silent, then the forest suddenly becomes magnificently real, and blazes transparently with the Reality of God. For now I know that the Creation, which first seems to reveal Him in concepts, then seems to hide Him by the same concepts, finally is revealed *in Him,* in the Holy Spirit. And we who are in God find ourselves united in Him with all that springs from Him. This is prayer, and this is glory![19] How did Merton develop these ideas about Creation as a window on God? Largely from the teachings of the Greek patristic writers, *theoria physike,* or "natural contemplation, which beholds the divine in and through nature."[20]

William Shannon, a major Merton scholar, notes that in much of his writing, Merton prefers the term "contemplation" to "mysticism" and sometimes uses the terms interchangeably. Yet Merton does not entirely avoid the term "mystic," and one of his works is entitled, *Mystics and Zen Masters.* We will return to Merton's ideas on mysticism when we consider the way of negation, for it was his preferred path to God; but we also must note that Merton thought the Christian contemplative should use both the way of negation and that of affirmation, in a balance or an alternation, recognizing that God would always be beyond any way or path which humans might pursue.

In fact, the word "way" or "path" is one of the most fundamental metaphors in the mystical life, worth our consideration as we develop an understanding of the progression and transformation which has come to be known as "the spiritual journey."

CHAPTER FIVE

The Soul's Journey

P̶eople of faith speak readily of their own spiritual quests as journeys. What is the source of this idea? Does it stem from biblical literature? Here let us also consult the experience of some early Christian mystics to inquire about the soul's descent from God, the loss of God, and the soul's pilgrimage of return.

A BIBLICAL MOTIF

No doubt Abraham's journey from Ur of the Chaldees to the land of Canaan can be regarded as the paradigm of the spiritual quest and the religious journey. God speaks directly to Abraham and makes a covenant with him. His journey made in the physical and geographic realm is also a spiritual adventure, a response of faith, a venture into the unknown, an act of obedience to the divine command. In a sense Abraham's journey prefigures all the journeys of the Bible: the travels of the Israelites in search of the Promised Land; the journey of the Magi in search of the Christ child; the hasty journey of Joseph, Mary and the child Jesus, usually called "the flight into Egypt;" the long walks of Jesus and his disciples to spread the kingdom of God; Paul's missionary journeys and those of other apostles throughout Mediterranean lands. These biblical journeys have no doubt shaped our picture of the religious quest.

In non-Jewish, non-Christian literature we also find the journey is part of rousing hero-stories: the adventure of Odysseus (*The Odyssey*); Jason and the Golden Fleece; and in a more sophisticated vein, *The Aeneid* of Virgil, in which one Trojan warrior travels far throughout the Mediterranean Sea until at last he becomes the founder of Rome. Whether historical or fictional, these are earth-bound (or seafaring) tales. Another journey motif has greater bearing on the mystical life: that of soul-journeys which transcend the earthly realm. Such soul-journeys occur on a higher plane: in dreams, in trances, in ecstatic or contemplative prayer.

Consider the soul-journeys reported in the apocalyptic books of the Bible.

In Daniel 7 we find that Daniel had a remarkable vision through a dream. Not only did he see four beasts, but also:

> As I watched thrones were set in place,
> and an Ancient One took his throne,
> his clothing was white as snow,
> and the hair of his head like pure wool;
> his throne was fiery flames,
> and its wheels were burning fire.
> A stream of fire issued
> and flowed from his presence.

A thousand thousands served him,
and ten thousand times ten thousand stood attending him.
The court sat in judgment,
and the books were opened (Dan 7:9-10).

This vision is of the last days, or the end-time, and in verses that shortly follow one like a human being comes and is presented to the Ancient One. This is the Son of Man, who is given dominion and power over all peoples, nations and languages. In the remainder of the Book of Daniel, Daniel receives the angelic visitors, Gabriel and Michael, and has other visions, suggesting a time of coming war and destruction associated with the last days.

In Revelation we find a close parallel.

> I, John . . . was on the island called Patmos. . . .
> I was in the spirit on the Lord's day and I heard behind me a loud voice like a trumpet saying, "Write in a book what you see and send it to the seven churches. . . .
> (Rev. 1:9–11)

And again in Revelation 4,

> After this I looked, and there in heaven a door stood open . . . . (Rev. 4:1). At once I was in the spirit, and there in heaven stood a throne, and one seated on the throne (Rev. 4:2).

And Paul, you will remember, found himself ("whether in the body or out of the body I do not know; God knows") caught up into the third heaven.

The history of Islam includes a famous account of Muhammad's heavenly journey, known as the "ascension." This ascension differs from that of Jesus, in which he is seen by his followers, after his resurrection, to be lifted up into heaven (which may indeed have been a mystical encounter for the apostles and witnesses to the event). Instead, the ascension of Muhammad can be described as a mystical experience for Muhammad himself: *In Introduction to Islam* by Muhammad Hamidullah (Centre Culturel Islamique, Paris, 1969) we read of this ascension:

> It was at this time that the Prophet Muhammad was granted the *mi'raj* (ascension): He saw in a vision that he was received in heaven by God, and was a witness of the marvels of the celestial regions. Returning, he brought for his community, as a Divine gift, Islamic worship, which constitutes a sort of communion between man and God. . . .
>
> The news of this celestial meeting led to an increase in the hostility of the pagans of Mecca;[1]

In short, the ascension ascribed to Muhammad was one of his many prophetic visions (the first one being an appearance of the Archangel Gabriel) which became the foundation of his teaching and which are gathered in the holy book of Islam, the Qur'an.

No doubt influenced by mystical prayer, accounts are given by early Christian mystical writers of soul-journeys which have as their basis the idea of a return to God.

This idea persists in contemporary religious language. The soul is imprisoned in the body. Human beings here on earth see themselves as being held in exile. In a famous prayer, the "Hail Holy Queen" addressed to Mary the mother of Jesus, Christians pray "in this valley of tears" and asked to be delivered from "this our exile." As recently as the 1800s the English Romantic poets wrote of such an exile, of the soul's removal from heaven to earth:

> Our life is but a dream and a forgetting;
> The soul that travels with us, our life's star
> Hath elsewhere had its setting
> And cometh from afar
> Not in entire forgetfulness
> And not in utter nakedness

> But trailing clouds of glory do we come
> From God, who is our home.[2]

The soul, plucked from heaven to earth, retains clouds of glory, Wordsworth says, only briefly. For soon "shades of the prison house begin to close about the growing boy." This idea, so prevalent among the British romantics, does not begin with them, it seems, but has its precedent in a much earlier mystical literature.

THE INFLUENCE OF ORIGEN

Origen (c.185–c.253) is an early and influential commentator on the soul-journey.[3] Born into a pious family in Alexandria, Egypt, Origen was trained both in the classics and the Hebrew and Christian Scriptures. He became a catechist and pursued a life of strong spirituality, spending night after night in the study of Holy Scripture. Under the patronage of Ambrose, Origen began to study and to write. He was ordained a priest, and after a dispute with Demetrius, then Bishop of Alexandria, he moved to Caesarea in Cappodocia, where the powerful effect of his teaching was recorded by Gregory Thaumaturgos, one of his pupils:

"And thus, like some spark lighting upon our inmost soul, love was kindled and burst into flame within us—a love at once to the Holy Word, the most lovely object of all . . . and to this man, his friend and advocate . . ."[4]

Origen teaches that the soul ascends to God through an encounter with the Scriptures. This upward journey is the essence of the Christian call, and is the main theme of Origen's mysticism. Before Origen can speak about the soul's journey upward to God, he first has to explain how the soul has come down from the higher realms.

Because of the fall of God's first creation there is now a second creation, in which we currently exist, where all is confusion and division. In the original creation our intellects were joined to God's in joyful contemplation. Now our minds are darkened, but even in our fallen state the freedom of the intellect remains. Our fallen intellects have three important levels: *pneuma*, or spirit, our connection to the Holy Spirit; *psyche* or soul, which is capable of contemplation if we choose that course; and *soma*, or the body, our material lives. In spite of the Fall, we have, in all three dimensions, a spark that makes us capable of regaining our original likeness to God. Jesus becomes for us the inspiration and model of how to do this, as well as the way by which such a reconnection is attained.

Scripture, the Word of God, is fundamental to this process. Origen mentions three Scriptural sources that trace the soul's mystical ascent. The first is Proverbs, which constitutes a school of virtuous living. The second is Ecclesiastes, the teacher who brings us enlightened knowledge of the nature of things. The third is the Song of Songs, that erotic encounter, so beloved by many mystics in many centuries. The Song of Songs, for Origen, is the full description of Christ's love for fallen humanity.

Origen gives us a clear image of Scripture as a spiritual path. If the soul journeys, as Origen claims, it is on a path traced by the Holy Word.[5]

Evagrius of Pontus

This notion of the soul's return, or journey back to God, comes easily to a number of early Christian writers and teachers of the mystical life. Evagrius of Pontus (c.345–399) is one of these major figures in Christian mysticism, whose life was not without controversy. (He is sometimes called Evagrius Ponticus; his surname, "of Pontus" means that he was born on the Hellespont, in the town of Ibora, in what is now modern Turkey.) After an involvement with a married woman he fled to the desert and took on a strongly ascetical life there.

Evagrius (whose spirituality has been controversial even in recent times)[6] takes over a number of Origen's ideas and elaborates on them. He is one of the first writers to speak of a journey that moves in stages. Evagrius believes that three stages are needed for the return of the fallen rational creation to its source in God. What are these three? One involves ascetic living. The second concerns contemplation of the physical world, and the third involves the contemplation of God.[7]

Two Parts Contemplation, One Part Action

Notice that there are two contemplative stages, one dealing with the natural world (Ecclesiastes, according to Origen) and one dealing with mystical contemplation of God. The ascetical life, or the pursuit of virtue, is seen as an active life. (*Askesis*, the Greek word for training, especially athletic training, gives rise to the adjective "ascetical" for training in holiness.) Evagrius is well-known for teaching this three fold division of spiritual transformation: two parts contemplation to one part action, a potent recipe.

Evagrius sets out principles for training in virtue, including a list of the passionate tendencies which may trip us up on the way to goodness. Among these evil thoughts and passions Evagrius lists impurity, greed, depression, impatience or dissatisfaction, conceitedness, and pride. It is by dealing with such tendencies that the soul is transformed, enough to enter into a contemplative way of living. The transformed soul is passionless: not so much without feeling, but not dominated by the passions and wicked thoughts. This more tranquil self can contemplate both the things of this world and of the next: corporeal and incorporeal beings. As a result, an unlimited contemplation of the Trinity becomes possible.

PARALLELS BETWEEN THE SOUL AND CHRIST

For both Origen and Evagrius, the return of the soul to God comes about through the incarnation of Christ. The platonic descent of the soul from God has a parallel: the descent of the Son into fleshly existence. Christ's return to his Father teaches us to follow him and return to the Father ourselves. While Evagrius does not use the language of "union" (it is common, but not universal terminology for the highest stage of mystical life) he nevertheless depicts a kind of reunion with the Godhead. He equates pure prayer with knowledge of the Trinity. Slowly, images and forms, all distractions, are stripped away. Mind and spirit directly attain knowledge of the Three in One. There is no intermediary, no intervening presence. "Prayer is the continual intercourse of the spirit with God."[8] The spirit has returned to God, the mind has ascended through the power of the incarnate Christ. "When minds flow back to him like torrents into the sea, he changes them all completely into his own nature, color and taste. They will no longer be many but one, in his unending and inseparable unity, because they are united and joined with him. As in the fusion of rivers with the sea no addition to its nature or variation in its color and taste is to be found, so also in the fusion of minds with the Father no duality of natures or quaternity of persons comes about."[9]

This fundamental vision of the mystic's return to God, established by Origen and Evagrius, will be continued by many of the early Christian mystical teachers, with fidelity, and with variations. John Cassian, Gregory the Great, Gregory of Nyssa, Augustine of Hippo, Dionysius the Areopagite, all speak of the soul's aspiration, of loss and return, descent from and ascent to God, return to the source of created life. Dionysius insists that the spirit's uplifting to God is brought about through the liturgical life, the life of worship and of community that is the church. The church, he says, points us to God in three ways: through a right understanding of Scripture; through the action of sacred rituals; through each one's proper place in the church. Even more important, Dionysius insists that our uplifting to God is not exactly an ascent. Instead, as we grasp the inner meanings of things, our knowledge and insight go deeper. The journey upward is actually a journey inward, into greater depths of soul.[10]

So it is that the language of the inner journey, of the soul's return to God, is taken up and elaborated, first by one and then another mystical teacher, until it becomes a well-known part of the language of Christian faith.

DANTE'S SOUL-JOURNEY

The poet Dante Alighieri (1265–1321) adds to this faith-language a vision of the human journey that encompasses all the received mystical teachings, in combination with the literary visions of pagan literature. Everything that Homer and Virgil had to say about the heroic journey is combined with the interior visions of Catholic Christian mystical life. In Dante's *Commedia*, Dante himself is a character in his own story. Lost, at mid-life, in a dark wood, Dante, the character, is met by Virgil, his spiritual guide, who takes him through the realms of hell and purgatory. At the far boundary of purgatory, a second spirit guide appears. This is Beatrice, who will take him into the realms of the heavenly paradise.

In Dante's story the notion of a transforming mystical journey is fully developed at last. This journey is both a descent (into the realm of the damned) as well as an ascent (up the mountain of purgatory) and an upward flight into breathtaking celestial spheres. Influenced by the geography and cosmology of his time, Dante depicts hell as an underground place, purgatory as a mountain, and heaven as rotating spheres peopled by angelic beings and saints. It is clear that with Dante the soul's journey is, as it had been with Origen, a mystical return to the blessed presence of God.

The love language of the mystical life is in full play here, and the imagery of heaven is rich and evocative. As Dante, guided by Beatrice, reaches the heights of heaven, he discovers a White Rose which is formed by circles and hierarchies of heavenly beings. Within these circles (to which Dante is introduced by Bernard of Clairvaux) are such admirable saints as Eve, Sarah, Rebecca, Rachel, Judith, Ruth, John the Baptist, Augustine, Francis of Assisi, and Benedict. Mary (the Virgin Mother) occupies the highest position in this saintly arrangement. Second to her are Adam and Peter, who holds the keys of the kingdom.

> But since the time left for your journey's vision
> grows short, let us stop there—like the good tailor
> who cuts the gown according to his cloth,
>
> And turn our eyes upon the Primal Love
> so that, looking toward Him, you penetrate
> his radiance as deep as possible.[11]

Throughout the *Paradiso* Dante's imagery is flooded with light: there are multiple orders of angelic and archangelic beings, shining hierarchies of holy persons, dazzling domes of stars, incandescent celestial spheres, brilliant images of roses and fire. Dante uses every conceivable poetic device, every metaphor, every ornament, to paint the divine vision, the mystical reunion of redeemed humanity with its source: the Three in One. He is dramatizing the soul's journey, the return from a fallen creation, through humility and surrender, through suffering and penitence, into the restored and redeemed kingdom of divine favor and love.

CHAPTER SIX

The Way of Affirmation

here are two ways of describing the mystical path: the negative, or apophatic path and the affirmative, or kataphatic path. Thomas Merton says that both are necessary, and that both ways are describing the same experience (an immediate encounter with God) in different terms.[1] Apophatic and kataphatic are corresponding but opposite expressions of a single phenomenon, just as the words "positive" and "negative" may correspond to one photographic image.

However, before we agree that the negative and affirmative ways are somehow "the same," we need first to know how they are different. Who are the practitioners of the affirmative way, and what sorts of experiences do they affirm?

Essentially, the kataphatic way affirms the presence of God in our midst, invisibly present in the visible world. The affirmative way is, at least partly, about finding God among his creatures and even *in* his creatures. Negative mysticism, in its simplest terms, is a move away from the world; while affirmative, or kataphatic mysticism, is world-embracing. "O World, I cannot hold thee close enough!" wrote Edna St. Vincent Millay. No mystic she, but Millay, a well-instructed Catholic and a woman of poetic insight, captures in these words a kataphatic spirituality of the world.

FRANCIS, AN AFFIRMATIVE MYSTIC

Francis of Assisi (1181–1224) seems to have practiced such a world-embracing mysticism. His spirituality of "Brother Sun" and "Sister Moon" suggests a deep affirmation of created things. Francis is known for his love of creation and of creatures. His love of animals is well-known; a story is told of how he tamed a wolf that was terrifying an Italian town.

Who was this simple man, and why has he become one of the most popular saints in Christian history? The son of a successful businessman in Assisi, Francis was something of a social gadabout, and became a soldier in Assisi's rivalry with another Italian town. Falling ill at this time, he soon began to discover his own interior life, and upon his return home had a remarkable experience in the dilapidated Church of San Damiano while praying before a small Byzantine-style crucifix. Francis heard God saying, "Go and repair my house, which you see is falling down." Francis did repair that church. But he also obeyed God's command at a deeper level. Following his religious longings and his sensitivity to the poor, Francis renounced his father's way of life, even his own clothes, and took up a religious calling, including voluntary poverty, prayer, and preaching. It was all about following the gospel.

Soon he had assembled a band of poor preachers who traveled far and wide in the service of Christ; eventually Francis had to turn his mind to organizational leadership and writing a Franciscan rule. But his whole life was governed by love of Christ (and Lady Poverty). Late in life Francis's intense prayer led to serious mystical encounters, and Francis received the stigmata. His life ended in blindness, botched surgery, and severe suffering. Franciscan spirituality gained enormous popularity in his lifetime and has never lost ground. Francis continues to be one of the best-known and most-loved among the saints.

DANTE'S COSMIC VISION OF LOVE

We have already mentioned Dante for his use of the spiritual journey as a motif. He is also a fine poet of the affirmative way, because he bases his masterpiece, the *Commedia*, on God's love revealed to him through the bodily beauty of a young woman, Beatrice, whom he has loved only from afar. Dante apparently fell in love with Beatrice Portinari when he was barely an adolescent. When she died in 1290, Dante (who was married to another woman, with whom he had four children) was desolate. He threw himself into the study of philosophy in an attempt to deal with his loss.

It is Beatrice who incorporates and incarnates God's love in Dante's eyes. Dante's poem (which he began in 1308, during a time of wandering exile from his native Florence) celebrates the affirmative way in other senses as well, for his description of spiritual realms is concrete, personal, and particular. In Dante's scheme the realms of the afterlife—hell, purgatory, and heaven—are peopled by distinctive personalities. There are no hazy figures in the realm of the damned but particular sinners whose wrongdoing is very human indeed. In the blessed realms Dante shows us men and women, saints and angels who reflect the beauty and power of their Creator. As Dante is carried upwards to the heavenly spheres, he is dazzled by the incandescent power of blessedness. God's nature is present in, and revealed by the communion of saints, the church triumphant. Such is the nature of the affirmative way, which leads its devotees into realms of glory.

Ignatius Loyola: Finding God in All Things

Still another notable mystic of the affirmative way is Ignatius Loyola, well-known for his teaching that God is to be found "in all things."

Ignatius Loyola (1491–1556) is one of the most influential religious founders in Christian history. The religious order which he founded (The Society of Jesus, informally known as the Jesuits) continues to have worldwide influence, and is especially known for its work in education and spiritual formation. Born at Casa de Torres in the province of Guipúzcoa, Spain, Ignatius became involved with affairs of court, as a page, courtier, and soldier. After he was wounded in the defense of Pamplona (one leg was wounded and the other broken by cannon fire), Ignatius recuperated, spending time reading the lives of saints. He began to make bold plans to live for Christ. He went as a pilgrim to Montserrat and made an all-night vigil, vowing to observe perpetual chastity and to live a spiritual life. During an extended visit to the Dominicans at Manresa, he cared for the sick, did penance, and prayed for long times in a cave. There, beside the Cardoner River, he had a mystical encounter with God.

Ignatius tried to visit the Holy Land, but was turned back at Jaffa because of the Turkish occupation. He returned to studies (philosophy, theology, and Latin) in Barcelona, Salamanca, and Paris. Interrogated and imprisoned for his opinions and later released, he earned the MA in Paris in

1534. By 1538 he had formed a group of spiritual companions who took vows of poverty, chastity, obedience, and loyalty to Pope Paul III. By 1539 the pope gave spoken approval to his group; solemn approval came the next year.

Other Jesuits were sent on far journeys while Ignatius remained at Rome, organizing, conducting vast correspondence, and doing apostolic work that included homes for orphans, catechumens, and penitent women. His *Spiritual Exercises* were approved by Paul III in 1538 and by his successor Julius III in 1550. In 1551 Ignatius opened the Jesuit Roman College with an attendance of 300; the German College soon followed. His *Constitutions* had a broad impact on religious life then, and later. Obedience was fundamental, but medieval practices such as praying in choir (mandatory prayers chanted in common), wearing a fixed habit, and obligatory penances, were done away with, leaving the Jesuits a freedom to enter into the contemporary scene.

Ignatius focused his energies on a spiritually renewed laity; his *Spiritual Exercises* were not to be read, but made, in intensive retreats pointed toward interior conversion. He himself was a contemplative, more taken up into mystical prayer as his life neared its end.

By contrast with the poetic vision of, say, John of the Cross (his contemporary and countryman) Ignatius seems very practical, levelheaded and earth bound in his instructions for living the spiritual life. Ignatius offers set meditations, including mental and imaginative re-enactments of biblical stories, mental prayer, examination of consciousness, and penitential practices. Ignatius's style of prayer is based on active use of the religious and spiritual imagination to heighten a person's sense of God's power and presence.

TERESA AND JOHN: TWO "WAYS" IN TENSION

Still another practitioner of the affirmative way is Teresa of Avila (1515–1582), who is known as a reformer, mystic, writer and a doctor of the church. Born into an aristocratic Castilian family, Teresa chose religious life as a Carmelite at age twenty, but experienced an interior conversion in 1555, at age forty. From then on she worked to re-establish the primitive Carmelite rule, including personal poverty, manual work, almsgiving, and a very serious regime of deep personal prayer. Teresa today is known for her writings, including her *Autobiography, The Way of Perfection,* and *The Interior Castle,* all of which are famous accounts of spiritual formation and the high reaches of prayer. Teresa was later declared a Doctor (learned teacher) of the Church.

As with Ignatius of Loyola, her style of prayer uses imagery (the interior castle with its seven dwelling places; water flowing in a garden). Such concrete but homely images serve to illuminate the nature of prayer and the nature of God. They are full of life and vitality, vivid and specific, in contrast to the obscurity mentioned in *The Cloud of Unknowing* or *The Dark Night* described by John of the Cross.

Since John of the Cross and Teresa of Avila were colleagues in the Carmelite reform, we can assume they were using similar forms of prayer. The techniques and methods of prayer, therefore, do not distinguish the negative and the affirmative ways. We may conclude that matters of personal disposition and personality have a part to play. A further conclusion is that God offers particular gifts of grace suited to each person who is drawn into contemplative and mystical prayer.

We have already noted that no mysticism is ever purely negative or affirmative. The two "ways" exist together (as Harvey Egan suggests) in a creative tension. Egan also notes the differing styles of prayer among the early Jesuits, with some happy to remain actively engaged in the world, while others required more silence and solitude. Some early Jesuits clamored for the hermit's life! Others, closer in temperament to their founder, managed their prayer in the midst of activity. There is no question that both Teresa of Avila and John of the Cross led active lives and carried major leadership responsibilities within their congregations—founding monasteries, acquiring and managing property, designing and building monastery structures, organizing country retreats and activities, traveling from one establishment to another, managing a large correspondence.

BROTHER LAWRENCE AND OTHERS

Surely Brother Lawrence of the Resurrection (1641–1691) belongs to the affirmative way. (We will treat him again in a later chapter.) He is known for a particular style of prayer that finds God in the present moment, in the middle of everything, one which he describes in his still popular treatise, *The Practice of the Presence of God*. His is a way of modest, unobtrusive prayer that connects with ordinary events.

Brother Lawrence's simple approach is to go through all the day's activities in awareness of God's presence. Because he spent time working in the kitchen, Lawrence jokingly referred to himself as "the lord of pots and pans." His prayer method was sublimely practical: "the time of business does not differ with me from the time of prayer; and in the noise and clatter of my kitchen, while several persons are at the same time calling for different things, I possess God in as great tranquillity as if I were upon my knees at the blessed sacrament."[2] A similar method of finding God in the middle of everything is professed by Thomas Kelly (1893–1941), a Quaker philosopher, educator and man of prayer who wrote the moving treatise, *A Testament of Devotion*. Frank Laubach (1884–1970) lived an amazing life of service in the Philippines. He offered some of his spiritual reflections in *Letters by a Modern Mystic*. These letters to his father describe a richer and fuller vision of the spiritual life, one that came to him as a healing balm after many personal trials. Ultimately he founded a world literacy program which took him (among other places) to Singapore, Ceylon, India, Egypt, Palestine, Syria and Turkey.[3]

PRAYING IN AND THROUGH THE PARTICULAR

Therese Martin, also known as Therese of Lisieux, had a way of praying within and through the ordinary things of life which is often called "The Little Way." She too, was a Carmelite, and in a very short lifetime developed a remarkable holiness and a deep friendship with God. Whether Therese Martin actually belongs in the affirmative way is subject to debate, for there are many elements in her spirituality that suggest the way of negation, a darkness in the way she felt Christ calling her. But her affirmation of God's presence in the small tasks and duties of her cloistered, Carmelite life, suggest a deep mystical joy in the middle of everything.

Gerard Manley Hopkins has already been mentioned as a mystical poet deeply influenced by God in the natural world. He, too, is a poet of the affirmative way. True to the Jesuit insight that God is to be found in all things, Hopkins wrote:

> I say more: the just man justices
> Keeps grace: that keeps all his goings graces;
> Acts in God's eye what in God's eye he is—
> Christ—for Christ plays in ten thousand places,
> Lovely in limbs and lovely in eyes not his
> To the Father through the features of men's faces.[4]

In this oft quoted passage Hopkins speaks of Christ present in others, many others. This gift, to see Christ in others, is mystical and belongs in the way of affirmation.

Perhaps the most striking mystic of the affirmative way in our own times is Pierre Teilhard de Chardin (1881–1955), the French Jesuit scientist and man of prayer who based a whole spirituality on Christ as the end point of a universe hurtling into the future. Teilhard, a paleontologist, attempted in many of his works to reconcile evolutionary science with the Christian understanding of creation and existence. Today, Teilhard's science has been set aside, but he is being increasingly recognized as a mystic.

Born in Sarcenat, France (the province of Auvergne); child of a devout Catholic family, he entered the Jesuits in 1899, studied in the United Kingdom and was ordained in 1911. He had met two major figures in paleontology and decided on this for his life's work, earning a doctorate from the Sorbonne in Paris. Teilhard also served as a stretcher bearer in Morocco during World War I. His work as a paleontologist led to travels to Central Asia, India, and Burma. In China he was involved with the discovery of Peking Man. After 1946 he worked principally in New York and Paris. Teilhard is known for two kinds of writing: first, his scientific writing, in which he proposed a large-scale theory of cosmic life ascending through humanity towards an ultimate Omega Point, or ending, in Jesus Christ; second, his spiritual writing. Needless to say, his scientific writing, with its joining of the physical and spiritual realms, was controversial. He was prevented by his religious superiors from accepting a professorship at the College of France; his work did not receive an imprimatur, or approval, by the Catholic Church for publication. Teilhard accepted these rebuffs; his writing, by and large, waited to be published after his death. Out of his full devotional life, Teilhard wrote a number of spiritual treatises. Among these, *The Divine Milieu* and *The Hymn of the Universe* are well-known.

Ursula King, a student of Teilhard's thought, has said that what is most central to Teilhard's spirituality is "a deep, intimate and extraordinarily vibrant love of Christ–the human Jesus and the Christ of the cosmos, the ever greater, ever present Christ, the touch of whose hands we encounter deeply within all things."[5] She sounds like a mystic herself! And she refers to Teilhard's own mysticism as "pan-Christic," in which his love of the world, shaped from early childhood's sense of an ever present God, and a deep reading of the mystics from his early days, are transformed into a perception of transcendence throughout the natural order.

Teilhard writes well about God's presence in our work. No doubt he is shaped by the affirmative Jesuit vision of God in all things. But he elaborates and connects God and work in a particularly insightful way. Teilhard describes "the divinisation of human endeavor." Also, he compares our work to the royal road of the Cross. "First, develop yourself, Christianity says to the Christian. . . . It is a truly Christian duty to grow, even in the eyes of men, and to make one's talents bear fruit, even though they be natural. . . . it is the collaboration, trembling with love, which we give to the hands of God, concerned to attire and prepare us (and the world) for the final union through sacrifice. Understood in this way, the care which we devote to personal achievement and embellishment is no more than a gift begun. . . ." Teilhard sees work in the light of Christ's teaching of sacrificial love. "And if you possess something, Christ says in the Gospel, leave it and follow me."

Teilhard speaks of this call to the Cross as a way of crossing a threshold:

> It is perfectly true that the Cross means going beyond the frontiers of the sensible world and even, in a sense, breaking with it. The final stages of the ascent to which it calls us compel us to cross a threshold, a critical point, where we lose touch with the zone of the realities of the senses. . . .

Towards the summit, wrapped in mist to our human eyes and to which the Cross invites us, we rise by a path which is the way of universal progress. The royal road of the Cross is no more nor less than the road of human endeavor supernaturally righted and prolonged. . . . [6]

"Once we have grasped the meaning of the Cross," Teilhard insists, "we are no longer in danger of finding life sad and ugly. We shall simply have become more attentive to its incomprehensible gravity." [7]

Teilhard thus raises up the Cross as a positive, not a negative symbol, pointing towards the transformation of humanity, human labor, and the created world. "To sum up, Jesus on the Cross is both the symbol and the reality of the immense labor of the centuries which has, little by little, raised up the created spirit and brought it back to the depths of the divine context." [8] This divine context, or in French, *le milieu divin,* is central to Teilhard's mystical vision. It is akin to Paul's, that "in Him we live and move and have our being." For Teilhard, words like *pleroma* (a New Testament term meaning something like "fullness") are commonplace and familiar. Teilhard sees and affirms God's presence in every material particle and in the far stretches of the universe.

We have seen how the affirmative way is lived out in the spirituality of a number of mystics. Now we turn to the so-called negative way, sometimes called the apophatic way.

CHAPTER SEVEN

The Way of Negation

ver time a language of darkness has developed in mystical prayer. There are many spiritual writers in this tradition. One of the best-loved handbooks of the spiritual life is *Abandonment to Divine Providence*, by Jean-Pierre deCaussade (1675–1751). DeCaussade writes: "The way of pure faith . . . enables us to find God at every moment. Can anything be more magnificent, more mysterious, and more blessed. . . . What has to be done to produce such an amazing effect? Just one thing: let God act and do all he wishes according to our state in life. Nothing in the spiritual life is easier, and it is within everybody's reach. Yet so wonderful and dark is this road that we need great faith to walk along it."[1]

Wonderful and dark is this road: such imagery is a strong motif in DeCaussade's writing. The imagery does not dominate him, but he seems to have accepted "the dark way" as part of his received vocabulary of spiritual formation. (The reader will note that DeCaussade is also, like Brother Lawrence, advocating a spirituality of the present moment. But in this case, his present moment is "wonderful and dark," requiring pure faith.)

This language of darkness, which remains influential today, is associated with the way of negation. It is a particular mystical understanding which rests on the ideas of hiddenness and darkness. How far back does this mystical tradition go?

According to Gregory of Nyssa, the tradition has biblical roots. In his *Life of Moses* he offers this commentary: "What does it mean that Moses entered the darkness and then saw God in it? Scripture teaches [that] as the mind progresses and through its ever greater and more perfect diligence, comes to apprehend reality, as it approaches more nearly to contemplation, it sees more clearly what of the divine nature is uncontemplated."[2]

In the Book of Exodus the biblical writer does not elaborate on the cloud of darkness in which Moses met God. But, Gregory of Nyssa does not hesitate to do so:

> For leaving behind everything that is observed...[the soul] keeps on penetrating deeper until...it gains access to the invisible and incomprehensible, and there it sees God.[3]

THE CLASSICAL TEACHING OF DARKNESS

Another classical source for this teaching of darkness in prayer is Dionysius the Areopagite who opens his *Mystical Theology* with the following prayer:

Trinity! Higher than any being
              any divinity, any goodness!
Guide of Christians
              in the wisdom of heaven!
Lead us up beyond knowing and light
              up to the farthest, highest peak
              of mystic Scripture
       where the mysteries of God's word
       lie simple, absolute, unchangeable

Notice the opening words of this prayer: "lead us up beyond knowing and light." The notion that God is beyond our knowing will become fundamental for this mystical path. Images of light and dark are intermingled:

       in the brilliant darkness of a hidden silence,
Amid the deepest shadow
       they pour overwhelming light
       on what is most manifest
Amid the wholly unsensed and unseen
       they completely fill our sightless mind
       with treasures beyond all beauty.[4]

Dionysius, you will remember, is an obscure Syrian monk, our earliest source for the word "mystic." Dionysius developed an idea introduced by earlier Christian writers: that God is beyond our comprehension. He enlarged this idea into a full scheme, a whole theology of the apophatic, or the negative, way.

THE CLOUD OF UNKNOWING

Possibly the best known mystical treatise of the negative way was written by an anonymous fourteenth-century English author, and is called *The Cloud of Unknowing*. This brief tract, of poetic density, is addressed to students of the spiritual life. Later mystics further describe this path, among them the

71

sixteenth-century Spanish Carmelite, John of the Cross. Twentieth-century writers and teachers of prayer, including Thomas Merton and Carlo Carretto, also embrace this tradition. For good or ill, metaphors of hiddenness and darkness have become widely known among students of spiritual life. Beginners and novices come to expect certain prayer experiences, using terms coined by the great teachers of prayer. Commentators elaborate on such experiences and embellish them. At times, negation seems to be the dominant theme of the spiritual life.

The author of *The Cloud of Unknowing* is writing in a definite tradition, but he also brings great freshness and clarity to his account of the mystical life. Little is known of him, though he is thought to be an English priest from the Midlands. He is clearly expert in the life of prayer. He speaks of such things as "a naked intent of the will," "a blind outstretching," "a gentle stirring of love," "a secret little love." It is clear that he wants to lead others away from conceptual knowing or cognitive thought about God toward a direct, personal, intimate encounter, so intense that it can only be captured in affectionate phraseology, a naming which is a kind of anti-naming, for sometimes the experience of God is simply called "it."

"Let your longing relentlessly beat upon the *cloud of unknowing* that lies between you and your God. Pierce that cloud with the keen shaft of your love, spurn the thought of anything less than God, and do not give up this work for anything. For the contemplative work of love by itself will eventually heal you of all the roots of sin."[5]

William Johnston, a twentieth-century spiritual teacher, perceives this fourteenth-century text as a radical departure from other works on the spiritual life in the same period. Many writers teach discursive meditation, in which a cognitive thought process is firmly in control. *The Cloud* author invites us to go in a radically different direction, Johnston says: "All thoughts, all concepts, all images must be buried beneath a cloud of forgetting, while our naked love (naked because divested of thought) must rise upward toward God, hidden in the cloud of unknowing."[6] The cloud of unknowing is above, between the meditator and God. And the cloud of forgetting is below, between the meditator and all creatures. In this in-between space, which is of course, no space at all, the meditator finds himself in the mystic silence (*silentium mysticum*) that Dionysius the Areopagite wrote about.

The author of *The Cloud* knows that what he is saying may confuse some readers, so he offers a caution against the literal interpretation of such terms as "in" and "up." "Still, I believe that great caution is necessary in interpreting words used in a spiritual sense so as not to be misled by the literal meaning. In particular, be careful of the words 'in' and 'up'. . . ."[7] The author of *The Cloud* has apparently confused his retreatants and novices by using spatial imagery to describe the high reaches of interior life. Such language of above and below, within and without, can easily become disorienting. He schools his readers on how to interpret these metaphors.

Most striking of all is *The Cloud* author's insistence that the person of prayer needs to be *nowhere*: "But to this you say: 'Where then shall I be? By your reckoning I am to be nowhere!' Exactly. In fact, you have expressed it rather well, for I would indeed have you be nowhere. Why? Because nowhere, physically, is everywhere spiritually."[8] Metaphors of nowhere and nothingness are fundamental to this author's experience of God. In the same passage he speaks of a "blessed nothingness" and tells us to "persevere in that nothingness." We are not to be concerned if our faculties fail to grasp it. This mystical encounter with God is beyond logic—beyond rationality. "It cannot be explained, only experienced."

Such notions of finding God by going beyond thought are especially appealing to moderns. And there are other ways in which *The Cloud of Unknowing* exerts contemporary appeal. Prayer instruction given by the author is similar to what one might hear in a retreat house today:

> If you want to gather all your desire into one simple word that the mind can retain, choose a short word rather than a long one. A one-syllable word such as "God" or "love" is best. But choose one that is meaningful for you. Then fix it in your mind so it will remain there come what may. The word will be your defense in conflict and in peace. Use it to beat upon the cloud of darkness above you and subdue all distractions consigning them to the cloud of forgetting beneath you. Should some thought go on annoying you, demanding to know what you are doing, answer with this one word alone.[9]

JOHN OF THE CROSS: THE DARK NIGHT

A further development of "the cloud of darkness" comes in the spiritual teachings of John of the Cross. John of the Cross is one of the most influential figures in the history of Christian spirituality, best known for his idea of "the dark night of the soul," or in some translations, "the dark night of the spirit."

John of the Cross (1542–1591) was a mystic, scholar, spiritual director, religious superior, and above all, a poet. Shortly after his ordination as a Carmelite priest John met and joined forces with Teresa of Avila, who was bringing about a revolution in Carmelite practice and spirituality. Teresa's movement was spreading through Spain like wildfire. Her contemplative communities were dedicated to a strict life of poverty, enclosure, fasting, silence, and, of course, a strong commitment to prayer. Teresa's Carmelites went barefoot as a sign of radical commitment to Christ. They were called Discalced Carmelites, Carmelites without sandals.[10]

Both Teresa and John were skilled organizers, planners and doers. Both were practicing the spiritual life at a deep level. As her spiritual director, John was able to shepherd Teresa through many intense mystical experiences. When Teresa's mystical journey reached a peak, John was a stabilizing influence. Both Teresa and John were on fire with love for Jesus, wise in the ways of church politics and religious communities; both kept calm under pressure.

John's love for the spiritual life was not a matter of shyness or introversion. A good conversationalist, expressive about his love of God, John was a spiritual director to thousands of persons, both in lay and religious life. But John's popularity as a spiritual director had its drawbacks. Others were jealous of him. Many of their fellow-religious conspired against Teresa and John—especially because of the mystical favors granted to them in contemplation. In 1577, John was arrested, blindfolded and imprisoned in Toledo. He had been accused of violations of monastic obedience by his fellow monks.

Confined to a room measuring six by ten feet, John was flogged, fed a subsistence diet, and held in solitary confinement, all common punishments of the time. He was pressured to renounce the Teresian way of life; but he refused. While he was detained, John continued to pray. He also composed poems which became the foundation of his distinctive spiritual teaching.

After his escape, John completed his literary work in more congenial surroundings: in the historic city of Granada, in a monastery overlooking the grandeur of the Sierra Nevada, and adjacent to the property of the Alhambra, the palace of the Muslim kings. But John never forgot his times of trial. He could always identify with the poor and the suffering, and followed the path of *nada*—nothing—in his passionate encounter with God. The poems begun in prison became essential to John's way of teaching the spiritual life.

John is justly famous for his idea of the "dark night." Most people engaged in spiritual life seem to grasp this idea almost without explanations. They have had their own times of trial and feel sure they know what John is talking about. But John's meaning may elude the casual reader. John gave to "the dark night" a specialized meaning, which has to do with purgation, or cleansing of the sinful self, by which one is drawn into prayerful, intimate union with God.

John speaks of more than one kind of dark night: the dark night of the senses is followed by the dark night of the spirit or soul. John's life-story suggests that he had certainly experienced what is commonly understood by "dark nights"—discouraging times when he was imprisoned and physically chastised—as well as mystical dark nights, in which the naked purity of the soul is laid open to God's transforming grace.

Because John is a poetic as well as an instructive writer, his terminology varies as he attempts to describe the development of the spiritual life. The term "dark night of the senses" is not used consistently or uniformly. Sometimes the term "active purification of the senses" is used instead. Also, the expression "dark night of the soul" is sometimes used inclusively—that is, "the dark night of the senses" seems to be part of, rather than contrasted to, the so-called "dark night of the soul." In still another place John refers to three dark nights: the night of the senses, the night of faith, and the night of the soul's union with God. "We can offer three reasons for calling this journey toward union with God a night. . . . The first has to do with denial of worldly appetites; the second has to do with the darkness of walking by faith; the third has to do "with the point of arrival, namely God. And God is also a dark night to the soul in this life. These three nights pass through a soul, or better, the soul passes through them in order to reach union with God." [11]

John's discussion of darkness is biblically rooted. He cites, for instance, Ps. 18:9b-11: "He set darkness under his feet.

And he rose above the cherubim and flew on the wings of the wind. He made darkness and the dark water his hiding place." He also cites the words of Solomon in 1 Kings 8:12: "Solomon then said: The Lord has promised to dwell in darkness." God was also covered with darkness when he appeared to Moses on the mount, John explains, citing Ex. 24:16. Then John mentions Job 38:1, 40:1, where God spoke to Job from the dark air. Paul is also cited (1 Cor. 13:10) to explain how the darkness of faith will yield to the light of understanding.[12]

The teachings of John of the Cross are deeper and richer than can be grasped at first sight. A shallow reading of "the dark night" suggests some kind of discouragement, or even (conceivably) depression. In fact, John's teaching should not be oversimplified. It is very close to "the cloud of unknowing" in that the soul, approaching God, loses its moorings, its sense of the familiar and the certain. But the dark night is more than a kind of disorientation. It is also a deep mystery of divine love.

By reading John of the Cross and others, we sense the mysterious depth of the mystic's intimate encounter with God. Also we discover that the mystics experience a progression in their spiritual lives. By consulting their writings, we too can come to trace the mystic path.

CHAPTER EIGHT

Tracing the Mystic Path

arly and medieval writers liked to teach
about certain predictable stages in the
mystical life. One such mystical treatise is
Walter Hilton's *The Scale of Perfection*,
sometimes called *The Ladder of Perfection*.
Hilton, (d. 1396) was probably an
Augustinian canon who spent the later part
of his life at the priory at Thurgarton in Nottinghamshire,
England. *The Scale of Perfection* was written for a devout
laywoman who wanted to practice contemplative life. Many
other writers appropriate Hilton's device, suggesting necessary
steps or stages in spiritual growth. In fact, because spiritual
writing from earlier centuries is generally framed as instruction,
heavy emphasis is placed on predictable passages—that is to
say, a set scheme—of spiritual transformation and development.

Teresa of Avila's books, *The Way of Perfection* and *The Interior Castle* both rely on the idea that spiritual life follows a certain arc. Her metaphors vary, but she suggests that the practiced and diligent person of prayer can anticipate beforehand how the journey to God will unfold.

Modern spiritual guides and writers challenge this approach, leaving more room for the work of grace and for personal individuality. They fear the confining effects of rigid, prescriptive schemes for attaining spiritual perfection. Nevertheless, there is a common language of the mystical journey. Certain stages seem to be generally acknowledged. Among these are (1) the awakening, (2) purgation, (3) illumination, and (4) union. Other recognized experiences are attributed to the mystical journey, intervening in ways that are less predictable. One of these is self-simplification or detachment, which may in fact be an aspect of purgation. A particularly notable experience is that of darkness, or the dark night of the soul/senses as described by John of the Cross. There is a danger in formulating these aspects of mystic path. Some who pursue the spiritual life may expect these stages to occur, and in a certain sequence. That risk, however, must be taken (with appropriate cautions) in order to mine the mystical literature and suggest the dynamic course of the mystic's journey. This is no once-in-a-lifetime awakening. It is sustained over time. The mystical experience does alter and change a person's life; nevertheless it is best described as an adventure, an on-going struggle, a journey.

In her study, *Mysticism*, the British scholar Evelyn Underhill gives a good account of some widely recognized stages, together with her sense of where mystical life is pointing, that is, what mysticism is *for,* where it leads, and what mysticism is all about. I propose to follow her general scheme, for she is not theological nor philosophical, nor essentially psychological in her viewpoint. She keeps a studied distance from the subject matter, yet she writes from the vantage point of belief. Mysticism is not, for her, a bizarre or paranormal subject, but rather an expression of the higher consciousness of humanity.[1]

The Awakening

What are the recognized phases of the mystic way? The first is the awakening, which might as easily be called a religious conversion. There are innumerable stories and studies of such an awakening, in which individuals feel summoned out of their ordinary existence into a direct meeting with God.

The conversion of Francis of Assisi is a good example. As we have seen, it took place in AD 1206 when Francis was twenty-four. For some time he had been wavering between the lure of the world and the call of the Spirit. Francis was dealing with what William James has called "the divided self." A high-spirited person of artistic temperament, he was also attracted by pursuits of war and self-indulgence. Legend has it, he "miserably squandered and wasted his time."[2] Yet Francis felt dissatisfied. While the celebrations were going on, he would begin to daydream and drop out, so to speak, of the festive spirit. Francis was also repelled by disease and ugliness. He gravitated toward beautiful things, music, dancing and the arts. But Francis felt another impulse drawing him to associate with beggars, to seek out and care for lepers, and to give way to charitable and self-humbling kinds of behavior.

After a few years of this ambivalence, Francis one day found himself walking in the country outside the gates of Assisi, and passed the little church of San Damiano. . . . "And, being led by the Spirit, he went in to pray; and he fell down before the Crucifix in devout supplication, and having *been smitten by unwonted visitations, found himself another man than he who had gone in.*"

So the first call to mysticism is in fact the experience of conversion. The struggle between two opposite ideals comes out in the open. A seemingly irrational impulse, the yearning for God, below the conscious level, breaks through and demands a commitment. Paul's language about the "old man" and "the new man" suddenly makes sense. This awakening brings about a marked contrast in the person and the personality. "He literally finds himself another man. He is as one who has slept and now awakes. . . ." Hundreds of such experiences have been recorded in Jewish and Christian history. In my own study, *Turning: Reflections on the Experience of Conversion,* I described this awakening in the lives of various modern people: C. S. Lewis, Bede Griffiths, Thomas Merton, Dorothy Day, Avery Dulles. Also, I told my own conversion story in brief. Reflecting on all six stories, I proposed four steps or stages in Christian conversion: desire, dialectic, struggle, and surrender.[3] Although Augustine of Hippo is often thought to be the paradigm of this awakening (perhaps because it took him so long to accept God's call) he is by no means unusual. This awakening may be more frequent than is generally understood.

Some awakenings are modest in tone. "There was no strain of music from within . . . when I was dragged through the doorway," C. S. Lewis wrote of his own conversion or surrender.[4] Underhill also takes note of mundane conversions. "[Sometimes] the revelation of an external splendor, the shining vision of the transcendent spiritual world, is wholly absent. The self awakes to that which is within, rather than to that which is without: to the immanent not the transcendent God, to the personal not the cosmic revelation. . . ."[5]

Whether an awakening be modest or exalted, a new sort of life comes into play, a level of engagement with God which did not seem to exist before. The person may recognize that he or she has been under God's direction all along, but a new kind of dialogue is now possible. Underhill calls this "a never to be

ended give-and-take" that comes to exist between the individual
and the Absolute. Though she uses somewhat abstract language,
she is speaking of a personal God. "The Spirit of Life has been
born: and the first word it learns to say is *Abba*, Father." This
is a vigorous dialogue, an active process. Life with God is vivid
and real. "The awakening of the self is to a new and more
active plane of being, new and more personal relations with
Reality; hence to a new and more real work which it must do."[6]

THE PURIFICATION

The second stage of the mystic way is one of purification
or purgation. While it may be painful, even a cause of suffering,
these are the growing pains of transformation. Underhill says
that "purgation is a privilege. . . . a dreadful joy. It is an
earnest of increasing life." In spite of discomfort and pain, the
mystic "recognizes in this breakup of his old universe an
essential part of the Great Work. . . . 'Let me suffer or die!'
said St. Teresa: a strange alternative in the ears of common
sense, but a forced option in the spiritual sphere." Underhill
mentions a similar passionate extravagance from Henry Suso
(Dominican preacher and mystic, c.1295–1366): "Teach me,
my only joy," cries Suso, "the way in which I may bear upon
my body the marks of Thy Love. . . .[7] We will hear more of
this passionate love chat when we consider the love language
of mysticism.

Great contemplative saints may pass through the stage of
purgation and purification, but in another sense they never
leave this stage behind them. As they come closer in an intimate relationship with the Almighty, their sins appear more
vivid to them. "In this sense, then, purification is a perpetual
process. That which mystical writers mean, however, when
they speak of the Way of Purgation, is rather the slow and
painful completion of Conversion. It is the drastic turning of

the self from the unreal to the real life: a setting of her house in order, an orientation of the mind to Truth."[8]

"The essence of purgation," says Richard of St. Victor, "is self-simplification."[9] (Richard of St. Victor's birth date is unknown. A native of Scotland, he was part of the mystical School of St. Victor; he died in Paris in 1173.) Another view of purgation is Thomas Merton's sustained reflection on the true self warring against the false self, a struggle which he himself never outgrew. He understood it as the fundamental issue of the contemplative life.

Strikingly, while Underhill speaks of necessary, successive stages of the mystic way, she is reluctant to say that the mystic moves completely from one to the next. Purification is on-going. Transformation is on-going. Self-simplification is a process that continues. It reminds me of John Henry Newman's insight (in his sermon "On Christian Repentance") that the most perfect Christian is ever but beginning, and comes home again like the prodigal son to be forgiven again and again.

DETACHMENT OR SIMPLICITY

Is detachment a stage on the mystic way? Or could it be an aspect of the mystic way throughout its progress? To flesh out an understanding of detachment, Underhill considers the so-called evangelical counsels: poverty, chastity and obedience.

> By Poverty the mystic means an utter self-stripping, the casting off of immaterial as well as material wealth, a complete detachment from all finite things. By Chastity he means an extreme and limpid purity of soul, cleansed from personal desire and virgin in all but God; by Obedience, that abnegation of selfhood, that mortification of the will, which results in a complete self-abandonment: a "holy indifference" to the accidents of life. These three aspects of perfection are really one. . . . We may therefore treat them as three manifestations of one thing: which

thing is <u>Inward Poverty.</u>" Blessed are the poor in spirit, for theirs is the Kingdom of Heaven," is the motto of all pilgrims on this road.[10]

Again, Francis of Assisi is a good role model for detachment or simplicity. "'My little sisters the birds,'" said St. Francis, greatest adept of that high wisdom, 'Brother Sun, Sister Water, Mother Earth.'" Underhill quotes Francis as follows: "'Not my servants, but my kindred and fellow-citizens, who may safely be loved so long as they are not desired. . . .' It is the business of Lady Poverty to confer on her lovers this freedom of the Universe, to eradicate delusion, cut out the spreading growth of claimfulness, purify the heart, and initiate them into the 'great life of the All.'"[11]

A more recent commentator on this detachment or simplicity is C. S. Lewis, who in *The Four Loves* clearly lays out the importance of a right ordering of one's loves, placing God always first, and everything else second or subordinate to the love of God.[12]

The mystic's detachment is a return to the liberty for which God made us. This liberation frees us from the domination of self. We return to a simpler way of living. Or as Augustine puts it in explaining the power of holy love: "Love, and do what you like." Underhill calls this "the most memorable and misquoted of epigrams."[13]

DARKNESS AND PURGATION

We have already looked at darkness as an aspect of the way of negation. Here we must also consider it as we trace the mystic path. The dark night and its analogues are part of the phase called purgation.

What does the image of darkness really mean? God is ultimately unknowable—dark—to our intellects. God uses this darkness to communicate with us all the same. [14] So we see that the image of "a dark night" or a divine darkness is not exclusive either to Dionysius or John of the Cross. It springs up, over and over, in the actual pursuit of the mystic way. "All these forms of the Dark Night—the 'Absence of God,' the sense of sin, the dark ecstasy, the loss of the self's old passion, peace and joy, and its apparent relapse to lower spiritual and mental levels—are considered by the mystics themselves to constitute aspects or parts of one and the same process: the final purification of the will or stronghold of the personality, that it may be merged without any reserve 'in God where it was first.'" Underhill insists that this darkness, this loss of consolation, has a purpose. It is "to cure the soul of the innate tendency to seek and rest in spiritual joys; to confuse Reality with the joy given by the contemplation of Reality." But notice. The Dark Night and its analogues are part of the way of purgation; darkness is cleansing us of our "disordered loves." What happens in this phase is "a total abandonment of the individualistic standpoint, of that trivial and egotistic quest of personal satisfaction which thwarts the great movement of the Flowing Light. . . ."[15]

Underhill interprets these "torments and desolations" as part of a "last and drastic purgation of the spirit."[16] It is all for the sake of bringing the contemplative heart closer to the love of God.

THE ILLUMINATION

Now we turn to the illuminative life, in which "a harmony is thus set up between the mystic and Life in all its forms. Undistracted by appearance, he sees, feels and knows it in one piercing act of loving comprehension." This new power of seeing seems at first to transform everything and offers the mystic "—perhaps for an instant, perhaps for long periods of bliss— an undistorted and more veritable world." Underhill locates the vision close to home: "The London streets are paths of loveliness; the very omnibuses look like colored archangels, their laps filled full of little trustful souls. . . ."[17]

This illuminated part of the mystic way is just what one might expect as the person moves toward transcendence . . . and a higher consciousness.

In my own description of the spiritual path, an account of the interior life under the influence of contemplation (*Clinging: the Experience of Prayer*[18]), I spoke of this stage as transparency. Transparency is that heightened consciousness—that new clarity of vision which comes about from the sustained experience of contemplative life. The Christian psychiatrist Gerald May has suggested that contemplation transforms the consciousness in a variety of ways, offering greater decisiveness, less anxiety, fewer distractions, greater focus. Surely these are an alternate vocabulary for simplicity and detachment. The aspect of seeing is what Underhill emphasizes for the illuminated way. My own experience confirms her insight. She speaks of the "cleansing of the doors of perception." As long as the reader understands that mystical consciousness is not consciousness-raising for its own sake, but rather for the sake of God's love, a claim of heightened seeing is no exaggeration.

In describing the life of prayer I avoided talk of stages or progression, mentioning instead moods and moments, aspects of the interior life. These moods I named as follows: *beginning, yielding, darkness, transparency, hoops of steel* (spiritual friendship or connectedness), *fear of heights,* and *clinging.* I learned later that "clinging" is the word used in Hebrew mysticism to describe intimacy with God: *devekut.*[19] My scheme, which I wanted to be non-prescriptive, can be seen as a close parallel to and re-interpretation of the historic mystical path: awakening, purgation, detachment and darkness, illumination, and union. But I did not copy from the earlier accounts. Instead, I made my own observations, attempting to use different, contemporary language.

Even so I must confess to Underhill's persuasive influence upon me. Today, her Edwardian terminology may sound somewhat old-fashioned, even antique. But compared to the earlier writers (Teresa of Avila, Thomas à Kempis, Julian of Norwich) she is modernity itself.

She insists for instance that the "illuminated mystic" does not live placidly. Life, for the mystic, is earnest and real. "Enlightenment is a symptom of growth and growth is a living process, which knows no rest. The spirit, indeed, is invaded by a heavenly peace; but it is the peace, not of idleness, but of ordered activity." And she cites Walter Hilton to support her claim: "'A rest most busy,' in Hilton's words: an appropriation of the Divine. The urgent push of an indwelling spirit, aspiring to its home in the heart of Reality, is felt more and more, as the invasion of the normal consciousness by the transcendental personality—the growth of the New Man—proceeds towards its term."[20]

WHAT IS THE CONTEMPLATIVE'S TESTIMONY?

What are these contemplatives telling us? They speak in contradictory ways. They mention simultaneously a dazzling vision and an abyss of emptiness. These are apparent, but not real, contradictories.[21]

Some may suppose that after Dionysius coined this idea of "divine darkness," writers since then have simply followed it, without examining or questioning the authenticity of his idea. Underhill opposes this, and I agree with her. "To argue thus is to forget that mystics are above all things, practical people. They do not write for the purpose of handing on a philosophical scheme, but in order to describe something which they have themselves experienced; something which they feel to be of transcendent importance for humanity. If, therefore, they persist—and they do persist—in using this simile of 'darkness' to describe their experience in contemplation, it can only be because it fits the facts. . . ."[22]

I fully agree with Underhill's view, because of my own experience in attempting to describe the moods and moments of contemplative prayer. When I wrote *Clinging* it was in order to describe what I had experienced; not to rephrase what the contemplative tradition had said to me.

The Unitive Life

Underhill romanticizes the unitive life as a loss of the self into the life of God. She takes that life seriously, but she fails, I think, at least in *Mysticism*, to emphasize the unitive life as one which continues in the middle of everything. In her later works, (*Practical Mysticism* and *The Spiritual Life* in particular) she is more down to earth. The unitive life is an intimacy with God which continues in the day-to-day course of our existence. Mysticism transforms, but does not take us out of the human condition.

Underhill's genius lies in seeing the clear relationship between the mystic path and our own. The mystics are kin to us, she claims. They may seem strange and far away, but they are not cut off from us. To interpret our own paths well, we need to reflect on our kinship with them. The mystics, Underhill says, belong to us. . . .[23]

Best of all, the mystics are pointing in the direction we all must go. They show us our destiny. "Waking very early they have run on before us, urged by the greatness of their love." Even though we are still not capable of "this sublime encounter," we can glimpse it by "looking in their magic mirror." By listening to the mystics, by looking at them, we "may see far off the consummation of the race."[24]

We can also learn from the mystics by sampling their intense love language, which gives us some hint of the exaltation which they experience. *Perhaps someday*, we say to ourselves, *we too may come to know God as intensely as they do.*

CHAPTER NINE

The Love Language of Mysticism

ystics speak extravagantly of their love of God. Their writing is often so lavish that the doubting Thomases of modern interpretation are suspicious of their intensity. How can this be godly love, when it brims with erotic passion? Never mind. The lush language of the mystics is the best they can do to speak of a love that is ineffable, unknowable, beyond imagining. In the Roman Catholic liturgy (drawing on biblical language) God is depicted as unapproachable:

> From age to age you dwell in unapproachable light;
> Countless hosts of angels stand before you to do your will.

Yet the mystic's claim is that this very God who dwells in unapproachable light is an intimate friend, a lover who lingers and dallies and keeps company with her or him.

Full of anguish that he has come to God so late in life, after such long searching, and after resisting a powerful summons, Augustine of Hippo writes:

> Late have I loved you, beauty so old and so new: late have I loved you. And see, you were within and I was in the external world and sought you there, and in my unlovely state I plunged into those lovely created things which you made. You were with me, and I was not with you. The lovely things kept me far from you, though if they did not have their existence in you, they had no existence at all. You called and cried out loud and shattered my deafness. You were radiant and resplendent, you put to flight my blindness. You were fragrant, and I drew in my breath and now pant after you. I tasted you, and I feel but hunger and thirst for you. You touched me, and I am set on fire to attain the peace which is yours.[1]

The extravagance of mystical writing gives us some hint—from the inside—of what mystics experience. Only the most articulate among them can put this into words. No doubt the ultimate reality of their experience escapes any full expression at all. Sometimes their poetry is so intense that we find it difficult to grasp.

These mystics speak of God as our Lover; and they speak of us as God's lovers. They are unabashed in the use of this intimate language. Julian of Norwich (c.1342–c.1416) was a British anchoress. She took vows to remain enclosed in order to pursue contemplative prayer. In 1373 when she lay close to death, she received sixteen revelations or "showings." After her recovery, her revelations were written down. One passage in her *Showings of Divine Love* reads as follows:

God shows the secrets necessary for his lovers; and how those who diligently receive the preaching of holy Church please God greatly.

Our Lord showed two kinds of secrets. One is this great secret with all the hidden points belonging to it. He wills that these secrets remain hidden. . . .

The second kind are the secrets he wills to make known and open to us, for he wills that we grasp that it is his will that we know them. They are secrets to us not only because he wills that they be hidden from us but also because of our blindness and ignorance. On these he has great pity, and therefore he wills to make them more open to us himself so that we may know him, love him and cling to him..

And then I saw that all is well.[2]

Richard Rolle (1290?–1349), a layman, spent about thirty-one years as a hermit, advising and directing others in the spiritual life. During the first six years he received unusual gifts, but refrained from describing them. He was afraid that these graces would disappear if he talked about them. He may also have wanted to avoid the usual church inquiries for people claiming unusual relationships with God. Rolle eventually did describe his passionate relationship to God, in a work called *Incendium Amoris*, that is, "The Fire of Love." Another great mystical work of his is called *Melos Amoris,* "The Song of Love." In both his Latin and English works Rolle is given to extravagant and poetic expressions of love: "O may Eternal Love totally develop our 'interior man' (Eph. 3:16) inflaming him with his sweetly flowing fire. May Love introduce him to a completely new glory and transform him into a true likeness to His own nature, as it were deifying him. . . . when his 'love is perfectly ordained' (Song 2:4) and his coordination is brimful of love, then 'all his heart, all his soul, all his strength' will press on to love God"(*Melos Amoris,* Chapter 50).[3]

LAMPS OF FIRE AND OTHER FIGURES

Another mystic given to extravagant language was John of the Cross. In his poetry he captured the drama and adventure of the spiritual life. Those around him clamored for explanations. So John's works—*The Ascent to Mount Carmel, The Dark Night, The Spiritual Canticle,* and *The Living Flame of Love*—are commentaries on his poems. The poems are inspired by Scripture, much of which John knew by heart. They also reflect the high drama and extravagant feeling of John's personal life.

John's poetry is rich in love language.

> Once in the dark of night
> When love burned bright with yearning, I arose
> (O windfall of delight!)
> And how I left none knows—
> dead to the world my house in deep repose;
>
> There in the lucky dark,
> none to observe me, darkness far and wide;
> no sign for me to mark,
> no other light, no guide,
> except for my heart—the fire, the fire inside!
>
> I stayed, not minding me;
> my forehead on the lover I reclined.
> Earth ending, I went free,
> left all my care behind,
> among the lilies falling and out of mind.[4]

John himself says that his stanzas "include all the doctrine I intend to discuss in this book, *The Ascent of Mount Carmel.* They describe the way that leads to the summit of the mount—that high state of perfection we here call union of a soul with God."[5] In *The Ascent* as well as in *The Dark Night* John deals both with purification and union. He explains to the reader that he will rely on sacred Scripture for his interpretations, rather than trust entirely to his own experiences.

The Spiritual Canticle, directly influenced by *The Song of Songs*, is a long poem. Imitating the biblical text, John writes a dialogue between two lovers, the bridegroom and the soul, who personify the Lord Jesus and his beloved. John composed (and later wrote down) the first thirty-one stanzas while he was imprisoned in Toledo, part of the lifelong persecution and harassment he experienced in religious life. But the poem expresses the deep consolation of his intimate love relationship with God, drawing on biblical imagery: mountains, valleys, rivers, flowers, caverns. John knew most of the Scripture text by heart. Many of his word pictures have become part of a kind of mystical language: "the wounded stag" (who symbolizes Jesus Christ, wounded by his love for us); and other striking images:

> My beloved, the mountains
> And lonely wooded valleys,
> Strange islands,
> and resounding rivers,
> the whistling of love-stirring breezes,
>
> The tranquil night
> At the time of the rising dawn,
> Silent music
> Sounding solitude
> The supper that refreshes, and deepens love.

His fourth major work, *The Living Flame of Love,* also based on a love lyric addressed to God, has similar spiritual energy:[6]

> O lamps of fire, whose light
> streams in the cavernous soul:
> through mighty hollows, dazzled from above
> (once dungeons) see tonight
> auroras pole to pole!
> lavishing warmth and brilliance on their love!

> How loveable, how loving
> you waken in my breast,
> stirring in nooks, no, none are sharers of!
> With your delicious breathing
> all health and heavenly rest
> how delicately I'm caught afire with love![7]

Teresa of Avila, like her colleague John of the Cross, is given to the language of lovers when she writes about her encounters with God.

> This prayer, then, is a little spark of the Lord's true love which he begins to enkindle in the soul. . . . [T]his little spark cannot be acquired. Yet, this nature of ours is so eager for delights that it tries everything; but it is quickly left cold. . . . If we don't extinguish it, through our own fault, it is what will begin to enkindle the large fire that (as I shall mention in its place) throws forth flames of the greatest love of God.
>
> The most important thing is not to think much but to love much; and so do that which best stirs you to love. Perhaps we don't know what love is. I wouldn't be very surprised because it doesn't consist in great delight but in desiring with strong determination to please God in everything, in striving, insofar as possible, not to offend him, and in asking him for the advancement and the honor and glory of his Son.[8]

THE METAPHYSICALS

The Anglican clergyman John Donne (1572–1631) is classed, along with George Herbert and several others, among the "metaphysical poets," whose work is known for its mystical character. Born into a Roman Catholic family, Donne was at first closed off both from university education and other preferments because of his religion. Later he became an Anglican, taking the necessary oaths to the Crown, and through the influence of King James I took holy orders and became a renowned Dean of St. Paul's Cathedral. Donne is known for the erotic tone of his divine poems. In fact, Donne wrote intense, secular love poetry during his youth to women he later called his "profane mistresses." Later, after a conversion experience, he expressed his love to God in an erotic way. Famous among his divine poems is

> Batter my heart, three-personed God; for You
> As yet but knock, breathe, shine, and seek to mend;
> That I may rise, and stand, o'erthrow me, and bend
> Your force, to break, blow, burn, and make me new.
> I, like an usurped town to another due,
> Labor to admit You, but oh! To no end;
> Reason, your viceroy in me, me should defend,
> But is captived and proves weak or untrue.
> Yet dearly I love you, and would be lovèd fain,
> But am betrothed unto Your enemy.
> Divorce me, untie, or break that knot again,
> Take me to you, imprison me, for I
> Except You enthrall me, never shall be free;
> Nor ever chaste, unless You ravish me.[9]

George Herbert (1593–1633) is another of the holy English poets who expressed his love to God with simple and passionate intensity. Herbert was born of a distinguished English family (who lived on the Welsh border). He had a fine career at Trinity College, Cambridge, (BA and MA) and might easily have chosen preferment at court. Instead he became a country parson, lived a short life, and became known as a major English mystical poet only after his death. Herbert played the lute and was extremely devoted to prayer. His closest friend was Nicholas Ferrar who had established a meditative community at Little Gidding, celebrated by T. S. Eliot in *Four Quartets*. Herbert has a sweet, artless way in his devotional poems; they bear his own stamp and show a deep knowledge of the inner life:

I cannot ope my eyes,
But Thou are ready there to catch
my morning soul and sacrifice;
Then we must needs for that day make a match.

My God, what is a heart?
Silver, or gold, or precious stone,
Or star, or rainbow, or a part
Of all these things, or all of them in one?

My God, what is a heart,
That Thou shouldst it so eye, and woo,
Pouring upon it all Thy art,
As if that Thou hadst nothing else to do?

Teach me thy love to know,
That this new light, which now I see,
May both the work and workman show,
Then by a sunbeam I will climb to Thee. [10]

One of the dearest commentators on love is the poet
William Blake (1787–1827) who is so often cited for these
lines:

And we are put on earth a little space
That we may learn to bear the beams of love.[11]

In his poem "The Divine Image" Blake writes:

To Mercy, Pity, Peace and Love
All pray in their distress;
And to these virtues of delight
Return their thankfulness.[12]

Christina Rossetti (1830–1894), an English poet, was the
daughter of a distinguished Italian political exile who became
Professor of English at King's College, London. Her more
famous brother, Dante Gabriel Rossetti, was also a poet and a

painter. Christina, a devout High Anglican, and a semi-invalid, was also known for her charities. In one of her best-known poems, "A Christmas Carol," Christina Rossetti expresses her deep love of God. Her poem looks beyond Christmas to the Second Coming of Christ, "when he comes to reign." She draws contrasts between heaven and earth, riches and poverty. Rossetti's devotion to Christ is shown intensely in her last stanza.

A CHRISTMAS CAROL

In the bleak mid-winter
   Frosty wind made moan,
Earth stood hard as iron,
   Water like a stone;
Snow had fallen, snow on snow,
   Snow on snow,
In the bleak mid-winter
   Long ago.

Our God, Heaven cannot hold him,
   Nor earth sustain;
Heaven and earth shall flee away
   When he comes to reign:
In the bleak mid-winter
   A stable-place sufficed
The Lord God Almighty
   Jesus Christ.

Enough for him whom cherubim
   Worship night and day,
A breastful of milk
   And a mangerful of hay;
Enough for him whom angels
   Fall down before,
The ox and ass and camel
   Which adore.

Angels and archangels
   May have gathered there,

Cherubim and seraphim
Thronged the air,
But only his mother
In her maiden bliss
Worshipped the Beloved
With a kiss.

What can I give him,
Poor as I am?
If I were a shepherd
I would bring a lamb,
If I were a wise man
I would do my part—
Yet what I can I give him,
Give my heart.

"THE MORE YOU MAKE US DESIRE"

One of the most extravagant lovers among the mystics is closer in time to us: Therese of Lisieux (1873–1897), who was canonized in the twentieth century. Much of her brief lifetime was spent in prayer, for Therese came from an intensely prayerful home and followed four of her sisters into the Carmelite convent. There she died young. Yet her mystical love of Jesus produced a striking autobiography, *The Story of a Soul*, which after her death made her world-famous. Known as "The Little Flower," she is among the most popular of Catholic saints.

It is said that in June, 1895, Therese took her sister Celine (who was in the same convent) to a little room adjoining her cell, knelt and read a formal statement of some 600 words in which she offered herself as a holocaust to God's love.

"I desire," it began, "To Love you and make You Loved. . . .

"I know, O My God! That the more You want to

give, the more You make us desire I feel in my heart immense desires and it is with confidence I ask You to come and take possession of my soul. . . . Remain in me as in a tabernacle.

"I want to console you for the ingratitude of the wicked. . . . If through weakness I sometimes fall, may your Divine Glance cleanse my soul immediately, consuming all my imperfections like the fire that transforms everything into itself. . . . in order to live in one single act of perfect Love, I OFFER MYSELF AS A VICTIM OF HOLOCAUST TO YOUR MERCIFUL LOVE asking You to consume me incessantly, allowing the waves of infinite tenderness shut up within You to overflow into my soul, and that thus I may become a martyr of your love."[13]

These are just a few examples of the passionate language of the mystics and mystical poets. One of the most popular of these was Francis Thompson (1859–1907) who, after his recovery from drug addiction, developed an overflowing love of God, which he expressed in his poem, "The Hound of Heaven."

> I fled Him, down the nights and down the days;
> I fled Him, down the arches of the years;
> I fled Him, down the labyrinthine ways
> Of my own mind; and in the mist of tears
> I hid from Him, and under running laughter.

In a series of thundering verses Thompson develops the figure of himself fleeing from the love of God, with God, the hound of heaven, in hot pursuit. It is clear that this chase has partly to do with the poet's need to forgive himself for the past, for the lost years, the things done wrong and the things left undone. His mangled youth lies dead, he says. But in the end everything comes together. The poet must also forgive God for the lost years and the hard times. And he does. God explains it all:

All which I took from Thee I did but take,
Not only for thy harms,
But just that Thou might'st seek it in My arms.
All which thy child's mistake
Fancies is lost, I have stored for thee at home.

The contemporary writer and speaker Richard J. Foster often elaborates these metaphors used by earlier writers on prayer. He paints a picture of God as an affectionate father who takes us tenderly into his lap, who invites us into the kitchen of his friendship. In every century, for those who are caught up intensely into the life of prayer, a language of deep affection begins to seem easy and natural, second nature.[14]

CHAPTER TEN

Mystical Gifts and Unusual Phenomena

nusual charismatic phenomena have sometimes been observed among the well-recognized mystics. Among these are the stigmata (Francis of Assisi and various others) and the gift of tears (Ignatius of Loyola and others). The gift of "reading hearts"—that is, knowing the thoughts of others without being told—is not uncommon. Some stories are told of influence over weather. Tradition tells us that Therese of Lisieux prayed for snow on her vow day, in August, and it snowed. A similar story is told of Benedict and his sister Scholastica, who met for spiritual conversation only once a year. Scholastica, wanting to prolong their visit, prayed for extreme weather and a torrent washed out the bridge and forced Benedict to make a longer stay in her company. [1]

More dramatic side-effects of mysticism include levitation and bi-location (being seen in two places at the same time). Locutions—hearing words spoken interiorly or out loud—are common among the mystics, and indeed may happen to anyone who is serious about prayer.

RADIANCE

A phenomenal radiance is sometimes observed among the mystics. Such a phenomenon or—"shining" recurs throughout biblical history. We are told that Moses came down from the mountain so transfigured, so bright that his face had to be veiled (Ex. 34:29). Jesus was transfigured in prayer (Mt. 17:2; Mk. 9:2). An unusual brightness was also seen in the face of the Quaker prophet, George Fox. William Penn spoke of Fox as having a "reverent frame."[2] More to the point, a gang of Cambridge students who made plans to harass Fox and rough him up, apparently refrained from doing so because of his shining face. "Oh he shines," they said, "Oh he glisters." And they left him alone.[3]

VISIONS AND APPARITIONS

Throughout religious history appearances have been recorded of divine beings and holy persons, conveying messages of one kind or another to humanity. These appearances are part of the lore of mysticism. The history of Catholic Christianity is rife with visions and apparitions, especially of Jesus, Mary his mother, Michael the Archangel, and certain saints. The Roman Catholic Church has recognized only a few Marian apparitions in the nineteenth and twentieth centuries, although there have been many. Our emphasis will be on documented material, and on the Church's extreme caution about bizarre phenomena.

One well-accepted apparition of Mary is the appearance at Fátima, Portugal, which happened six times between May 13 and October 13, 1917.

There, in the rural locale of Cova da Iria (in a natural depression) three shepherd children, Lucia dos Santos (1907-) and her cousins Francisco (1908–1919) and Jacinta (1910–1920) saw a figure of a lady brighter than the sun, standing on a cloud in an evergreen tree. All three children saw the figure. Only the two girls heard her voice. The lady asked the children to return to the same place on the thirteenth of each month until October, when she would reveal her identity and make her requests known to them. This first event resulted in much local disbelief. Each month the children returned to the spot. The accompanying crowds swelled in number. In June there were 50 persons, in July 1,000, in August 18,000, in September 30,000, and in October 50,000.

There were many anticlerical journalists and activists in Portugal during that time. They created a firestorm of resistance to the Fátima appearances. On August 13 the civil prefect of Outrem kidnapped the children and held them, subjecting them to threats and interrogation for two days. But the lady appeared to them on August 19, promising them that a great miracle would take place in October.

In the October appearance, during wet and overcast weather, the lady told the children she was Our Lady of the Rosary. She asked for amendment in people's lives. Then the sun appeared and seemed to tremble, rotate violently, and fall towards the assembled crowds. The sun was said to dance. This "miracle of the sun" was repeated twice more and seen by a number of witnesses. After these events some members of the press became less hostile in their coverage.

A formal church inquiry began in 1922 and lasted seven years. In 1930 a local bishop said that the Fátima visions should be believed. Two of the children died young; Lucia lived a long life as a nun, entering a Carmelite monastery in 1948. She was able to provide detailed accounts of her conversations with the lady, along with new information on angelic appearances during the year 1915. The Pope became the guardian of the Fátima information throughout the twentieth century. Mary, in the vision, had asked for prayers for the conversion of Russia, which had fallen prey to atheistic Communism. The Fátima information, long held secret by the Pope, was recently made public because of the Vatican's concerns that unrealistic endtime speculations were being fueled by secrecy. Cova de Iria has been paved over. The Basilica of Our Lady of Fátima, a major structure with an imposing high tower, stands there. Nearby, on the site of the tree where the apparitions were first seen, is the Chapel of the Apparition. After the fall of Soviet Communism many believers attributed that political event to Mary's intercession. Today, the Fátima scene continues as a place of pilgrimage for believers and curiosity seekers alike.

LEVITATION

Herbert Thurston, an authority on the unusual phenomena of mysticism, is often dubious about strange tales in the lives of saints. In his exhaustive study, *The Physical Phenomena of Mysticism,* he questions and doubts many accounts of levitation in the lives of such notables as Francis of Assisi and Dominic. "The plain facts from which we cannot escape seem to be these: first, that down to 1260, thirty-four years after the Saint's death, we hear no word about any sort of physical levitation; secondly, that St. Bonaventure before 1266 states very simply that in prayer St. Francis was often radiant with light and raised from the ground; thirdly, that a later generation, certainly before 1320, declared that he soared to the tree tops and almost disappeared from view."[4] Thurston attributes the latter to extravagant piety, rather than definitive evidence. He also notes that the Latin word *suspendebatur* can mean "he was suspended" or else "he was entranced." Thurston thinks the latter meaning more plausible, especially in the absence of any contemporary witnesses to such suspensions. In the case of St. Dominic, Thurston alleges, the case is similar. Although later authorities claim that Dominic was raised by "several palms" above the ground, his contemporaries who gave accounts of observing him in prayer spoke of groans, sighs, devotion and penitence, but never mentioned his being raised in the air. Mention of uplifting creeps into Dominic's biographies fifty years after his death. Thurston also doubts the levitation attributed to Ignatius of Loyola and Francis Xavier, on exactly the same grounds. The people who knew them best, and gave formal depositions for the canonization process, never mentioned any such thing.

Yet Thurston is willing to accept some kinds of evidence. Teresa of Avila is a case in point. In her autobiography she speaks of the difference between union and rapture. Rapture, she says, is completely irresistible. "It comes, in general, as a shock, quick and sharp, before you can collect your thoughts, or help yourself in any way, and you see it and feel it as a cloud, or a strong eagle rising upward and carrying you away with its wings." Teresa makes clear that she is not just speaking of a trance, but also of being lifted up in the air: "My soul was carried away, and almost always my head with it–I had no power over it–and now and then the whole body as well, so that it was lifted up from the ground." On similar occasions Teresa is said to have clutched at the bars of the grille, or another time to have seized floor mats (*esteras*) in an effort to slow down or stop the rapture and levitation.

An incident is related by Bishop Yepes who was Teresa's contemporary; he knew Teresa well. Apparently Bishop Alvaro de Mendoza was giving communion to the Carmelite nuns at their *comulgatorio* (the aperture through which the cloistered women received the sacrament) and Teresa was unable to receive the sacrament because she had been lifted up above the range of the aperture. Teresa herself gives an account of this event and the difficulties ("sore distress") it caused her, and how she frequently asked the Lord to refrain from giving her these favors; and how the favors made her afraid.

> It seemed to me, when I tried to make some resistance, as if a great force beneath my feet lifted me up. . . . I confess that it threw me into great fear, very great indeed at first; for in seeing one's body thus lifted up from the earth, though the spirit draws it upward after itself . . . the senses are not lost; at least I was so much myself as to be able to see that I was being lifted up. . . . After the rapture was over, I have to say that my body seemed frequently to be buoyant, as if all weight had departed from it, so much so that now and then I scarcely knew that my feet touched the ground.[5]

Thurston cites this passage from a facsimile of Teresa's own autograph copy, submitted to the censors of the Inquisition during her lifetime. The document was completed in 1566. The Inquisitor's approval was given in 1575. During inquiries made after her death, a modest number of witnesses gave evidence of having seen Teresa raised from the ground in ecstasy. One of these was Sister Anne of the Incarnation at Segovia who testified under oath.

> On another occasion between one or two o'clock in the daytime I was in the choir waiting for the bell to ring when our holy Mother entered and knelt down for perhaps the half of a quarter of an hour. As I was looking on she was raised about half a yard from the ground without her feet touching it. At this I was terrified, and she, for her part, was trembling all over. So I moved to where she was and I put my hands under her feet, over which I remained weeping for something like half-an-hour while the ecstasy lasted.

When Teresa came to herself she asked Sister Anne to say nothing about what she had seen.

Thurston gives additional plausible accounts of levitation observed by others and accompanied by first person narratives: Sister (Suor) Maria Villani, a seventeenth-century Dominican nun, St. Catherine of Siena, St. Mary Magdalen of Pazzi, and St. Philip Neri. The most bizarre example he mentions is St. Joseph of Cupertino, whose strange levitations and flights were observed more than a hundred times. A number of witnesses testified about these curious events. St. Joseph's levitations often began with a shrill cry; he passed over the heads of congregations, leaving observers amazed; took hold of holy objects, such as a statue of the Infant Jesus, and carried them with him through his wild flights; even, on one occasion, he is said to have taken hold of another friar, lifting him along for the ride. Eyewitnesses were deposed only two years after the saint's death.

Similar stories are told about the ecstatic St. Peter de Alcantara, whose flights resembled those of Joseph of Cupertino. They were surprising movements across significant distances, beginning with a sudden shriek or cry which aroused fear, not devotion, among those present.[6]

STIGMATA OR "WOUNDS OF CHRIST"

Francis of Assisi is apparently the first person who experienced the stigmata. However, since his time, many examples of this phenomenon are recorded, the most notable recent example being Padre Pio (see Chapter 1) who has been canonized in recent years. A second twentieth-century mystic who received the stigmata is more controversial: Therese Neumann (1898–1964), a peasant woman of Bavaria. In March 1926 she experienced for the first time open wounds on the back of each hand and on the instep of each foot. These wounds became active only on Fridays, when they bled profusely. On Good Friday of each year she bled from her hands, feet, side, eyes, head and shoulder; she was experiencing the passion and death of Christ in a religious ecstasy. However, this was not the only remarkable claim made about Therese Neumann. Beginning in 1923 she began to subsist entirely on liquids. In 1927 she gave up both food and water entirely, her only food being the consecrated wafer of holy communion. She maintained this for thirty-five years. Neumann had been very sick for seven years prior to the onset of her charismatic manifestations. She had also experienced blindness. However, she had interior visions of St. Therese of the Child Jesus (Therese of Lisieux, whom she regarded as her patron saint). On the feast days of St. Therese, her namesake, Therese Neumann had spontaneous improvements in her health. On April 29, 1923, her sight returned. She told an interviewer that this spontaneous return of her vision took place on "The same day that Pope Pius XI declared me to be 'blessed.'"[7]

Psychologists tend to explain such unusual phenomena as aspects of high-strung, nervous personalities. In fact, many so-called "miraculous" phenomena of the mystics can be dismissed either as nervous conditions or else as the stuff of pious legend. But on the whole, the Roman Catholic Church is also very stringent in its investigations and conducts inquiries with sworn testimony. All of this testimony is less easily dismissed.

MULTIPLICATION OF FOOD AND LIKE MATTERS

The story told in the Gospels of Jesus feeding the five thousand has its parallels in the lives of later mystics and prayerful communities.

St. Andrew Hubert Fournet, the founder and mentor of a little known congregation of women, the Daughters of the

Cross, was canonized on June 4, 1933, in Rome, as Herbert Thurston relates, "with all the usual solemnities." Sr. Bartholemew, one of his group, who worked in poverty with the largely poor peasants of Western France, gave the following evidence in the inquiry for his beatification:

> While I was still at La Puye, there was committed to my charge the care of the granary and of the laundry. It was, so far as I can remember, 1824–before the feast of John the Baptist. We were looking forward to the annual retreat . . . when our good Mother Elizabeth [the Venerable Foundress, Elizabeth Bichier] told Father Andrew that it was impossible for that year . . . because we had not corn enough in the house and there was no money to buy more. The Father answered, "My child, where is your faith? Do you think God's arm is shortened, and that He cannot do here what he did of old when, as we read in the Gospels, He multiplied the loaves? Go and write the Sisters to come to the retreat."[8]

The witness described having seen the good father, Andrew Fournet, with his manservant, come to the granary and pray for an increase of the corn. There were two heaps which she judged to be inadequate for the crowd of sisters who would come to the retreat. Without any visible increase in the two heaps, the sisters did come and there was a more than adequate supply of food. Other testimonies from other community members were given to the same effect.

Herbert Thurston mentions other saints in whose lives such things happened and were authenticated by the testimony of others. He also cites the treatise by Pope Benedict XIV on the beatification and canonization of saints, in which such cases were noted in the lives of: St. Clare of Assisi, St. Richard of Chichester, St. Teresa of Avila, St. Frances of Rome, St. Mary Magdalen of Pazzi, St. Pius V, St. Rose of Lima, St. Aloysius Gonzaga, St. Francis Xavier, St. Cunegund, and St. Elizabeth, Queen of Portugal, among others.

A very recent account of the multiplication of food is related in the documentary film, "Viva Cristo Rey" which is an account of a charismatic community in Texas on the border of Mexico which ministers to the poor. This community, which was established by a deeply prayerful Jesuit priest, had an experience of the multiplication of food when on a holiday, they set out to feed destitute families, but had fewer meals on hand than the number of those who came for food. In ways that the eyewitnesses could not account for, everyone present was fed, and leftovers were saved. Their moving account seems well-attested; it is a direct parallel to Gospel events.

OTHER UNUSUAL PHENOMENA

What other odd phenomena have been associated with mystics? Some of these, such as luminosity, have already been mentioned. Others will be briefly noted here. They are: tokens of espousal, in which various saints have received the marks of wedding rings on their ring fingers, indicating a mystical marriage; bodily elongation during ecstasy; and *incendium amoris*, or "the fire of love" in which time spent passionately in prayer results in elevated body temperatures. After-death phenomena have also been observed, such as the "odor of sanctity," a sweet smell occurring in the presence of a holy person while dying or after death; incorruption of the dead bodies of holy persons, attested to in official exhumations; and the absence of rigidity in their cadavers.

Why is the Roman Catholic Church so ambivalent about these phenomena? I think it is precisely because Roman Catholics do believe in the miraculous. Therefore, they do not want remarkable events to be cheapened or distorted by charlatanism, or by the superstitious miracle-seeking of ignorant, pious people. Since Vatican II, efforts have been made to de-mythologize the records of the saints. Catherine of

Alexandria, for example, has long been a figure of popular piety. Now events in her life are thought to be legendary. The story of St. Christopher's encounter with the Christ-Child is thought to be a pious fiction; it once was considered a historical event. Questions have been raised about such well-established Marian appearances as Our Lady of Guadalupe, although the Roman Catholic Church has validated the vision by establishing a new feast of Our Lady of Guadalupe on December 12.

Spiritual Gifts as Burdens

Should mystics desire unusual or charismatic gifts? We have already noted Paul the Apostle's caution against such a desire. A vivid caution is also provided by Ignatius of Loyola, who received the mystical gift of tears. The gift of tears is not merely an occasional bout of crying. It is sustained weeping which affects the eyesight and endangers one's capacity to live in a normal manner. Francis of Assisi welcomed this gift, but Ignatius attempted for years to stave it off. Eventually he could resist it no longer. In a letter to a priest of his own Society of Jesus who had inquired about the gift of tears, Ignatius wrote the following:

"Some indeed have tears naturally, when the higher motion of the soul makes itself felt in the lower, or because God our Lord, seeing that it would be good for them, allows them to melt into tears. But this doesn't mean that they have greater charity or that they are more effective than others who enjoy no tears."

Then Ignatius explained his genuine feelings to his brother-priest:

"Even if it were in my power to give this gift to you, I wouldn't. It wouldn't help your charity; and it might even be harmful both to your head and your health; that's to say, it stands in the way of every act of charity. So don't lose heart just because your eyes haven't turned into spigots."[9]

Suffice it to say, spiritual gifts, especially bizarre phenomena, are not to be coveted by believers in general, nor by those so advanced in prayer that they are called mystics. The mystics themselves who receive such gifts do not, at least consciously, cultivate or desire them. They are the first to protest against their importance. In this matter the recognized mystics of the Christian church give to the rest of the faithful a very good example.

CHAPTER ELEVEN

Group Mysticism

any Christian communities over time have experienced mystical gifts in common. The Quaker communities of the seventeenth century are good examples. In the twentieth and twenty-first centuries, Pentecostal and Charismatic groups in the United States have testified to the influence of the Holy Spirit.

WHAT IS THE CHARISMATIC TRADITION?

The Charismatic tradition considers itself a life immersed in, empowered by, and under the direction of the Spirit of God. It is viewed, by those who pursue it, as a way of being empowered by God to do his work and evidence his life on earth.

Charismatic Christians pray for the influence of the Holy Spirit in their lives. They invite the Holy Spirit to be part of their prayer lives. They ask the Holy Spirit to dwell in them, and to pray through them. Sometimes they do this singly; but often they pray in groups. When making decisions they listen to the Advocate (one of many titles for the Holy Spirit; other common titles are the Helper, the Comforter, and the Paraclete).

Because of their sincere attentiveness to the Holy Spirit, charismatic communities often manifest the same gifts mentioned in the New Testament. Among these are healing, the gift of speaking in tongues, prophecy, and discernment of spirits. In recent years many such gifts have become so pronounced as to be controversial. Southern Baptist churches have prohibited speaking in tongues. The so-called "Toronto blessing," of prolonged uncontrollable laughter, has been widely disputed as to its authenticity.

The early Christian communities gave evidence of a collective ecstatic experience. A vivid account of this is given in the Acts of the Apostles (Acts 2). "When the day of Pentecost had come, they were all together in one place. And suddenly from heaven there came a sound like the rush of a violent wind, and it filled the entire house where they were sitting. Divided tongues, as of fire, appeared among them, and a tongue rested on each of them. All of them were filled with the Holy Spirit and began to speak in other languages, as the Spirit gave them ability" (Acts 2:1–4). It is not certain that this particular gift of tongues was the *glossolalia* with which we are still familiar in charismatic groups today, for the "languages" spoken by the gathered community were recognized languages known to many at the time. "Now there were devout Jews from every nation under heaven living in Jerusalem. And at this sound the crowd gathered and was bewildered, because each one of them heard them speaking in the native language of each. Amazed and astonished, they asked, 'Are not all of these who

116

are speaking Galileans? And how is it that we hear, each of us, in our own native language?'" (Acts 2:5-6). Later in the passage Peter has to defend their behavior. "Indeed," he explains, "these are not drunk, as you suppose, for it is only nine o'clock in the morning" (Acts 2:15). Peter insists that their ecstasies are a fulfillment of the prophecy of Joel: "And your sons and your daughters shall prophesy, and your young men shall see visions, and your old men shall dream dreams" (Acts 2: 17).

THE CHARISMATIC APOSTLES

Similar evidences of the Holy Spirit continued in the early apostolic church. Paul's first missionary journey to Cyprus is a case in point. Barnabas and Saul, who had been working in Antioch for a year, were specially commissioned by the Holy Spirit to go to Cyprus. When they arrived, the Pro-consul of the Island, Sergius Paulus, invited them to speak at the palace. But one man, Bar-Jesus or Elymas by name, tried to stop them. Paul, filled with the Holy Spirit, said, "The hand of the Lord is against you, and you will be blind for awhile, unable to see the sun" (Acts 13:9,11). And the man was struck blind. This incident (in which blindness has both a literal and a symbolic meaning) parallels the events of Paul's own conversion, when he was struck blind during a vision of Jesus on the Damascus Road.

Paul's second journey to Philippi involved an exorcism. "There stood a man of Macedonia pleading with him and saying, 'Come over to Macedonia to help us'" (Acts 16:9). Upon arriving in Philippi, Paul, Silas, Timothy and Luke began by joining a prayer gathering of women down by the river (Acts 16:13). Lydia was converted and invited the apostles to stay in her home (Acts 16:14-15).

One event involving Paul's charismatic gifts is related in Acts 16. A young slave girl who had a spirit of divination cried out . . . Paul cast out the demon possessing this slave girl (Acts 16:18).

But her owners, who apparently had been profiting from the slave girl's malady, were not happy; Paul and Silas were beaten and imprisoned on a trumped-up charge. Then the Holy Spirit intervened, causing an earthquake that opened the prison doors; the jailer asked to become a Christian (Acts 16: 26–34).

Paul's third missionary journey was to Ephesus. There, his extended preaching led to many miraculous healings. Luke records in Acts that healings occurred, not only when Paul was present and laid hands on the sick, but also when cloth objects *which had touched Paul's skin* were applied to those who were sick.

Needless to say, these charismatic gifts produced sudden and widespread conversions among the people of various Middle Eastern and Mediterranean locales.

> Now those who were scattered went from place to place, proclaiming the word. Philip went down to the city of Samaria and proclaimed the Messiah to them. The crowds with one accord listened eagerly to what was said by Philip, hearing and seeing the signs that he did, for unclean spirits, crying with loud shrieks, came out of many who were possessed; and many others who were paralyzed or lame were cured. So there was great joy in that city. Then an angel of the Lord said to Philip, "Get up and go toward the south to the road that goes down from Jerusalem to Gaza." (This is a wilderness road.) So he got up and went.
>
> Now there was an Ethiopian eunuch, a court official of the Candace, queen of the Ethiopians, in charge of her entire treasury. He had come to Jerusalem to worship and was returning home; seated in his chariot, he was reading the prophet Isaiah. Then the Spirit said to Philip, "Go over to this chariot and join it." So Philip ran up to it and heard him reading the prophet Isaiah. He asked, "Do you understand what you are reading?" He replied, "How can I, unless someone guides me?" And he invited Philip to get in and sit beside him. Then Philip began to speak, and

starting with this scripture, he proclaimed to him the good news about Jesus. As they were going along the road, they came to some water; and the eunuch said, "Look, here is water! What is to prevent me from being baptized?" He commanded the chariot to stop, and both of them, Philip and the eunuch, went down into the water, and Philip baptized him. When they came up out of the water, the Spirit of the Lord snatched Philip away; the eunuch saw him no more, and went on his way rejoicing (Acts 8:4–8, 26–31, 35–39).

Angelic appearances, divine guidance, sudden conversions, speaking in tongues: it's little wonder that the new Christian church made headway in spite of persecution and imprisonment. As we have noted earlier, Paul was conscious of having remarkable charismatic gifts, including the gift of tongues (First Letter to the Corinthians). But he insists that Christians should not envy these gifts or take pride in having them.

Throughout Christian history, there have been many charisms within churches. There have also been many cases where a powerful charism was rejected by traditional Christian churches, causing new groups to form. The twentieth century is equally remarkable along these lines. Between 1895 and 1903 Blessed Sister Elena Guerra, who founded the Oblate Sisters of the Holy Spirit in Italy, wrote twelve confidential letters to Pope Leo XIII, asking him to foster devotion to the Holy Spirit within the Catholic church. Pope Leo XIII received her request warmly. He asked for the whole church to celebrate a solemn Novena (a sequence of nine days of prayer and devotion), asking for an outpouring of the Holy Spirit. On October 15, 1900, she wrote again, suggesting that he begin the new century with the hymn, *"Veni Creator Spiritus,"* ("Come, Holy Spirit") in the name of the whole Catholic Church. The Pope did so on New Year's Day, 1901, at St. Peter's Basilica in Rome.

Interestingly, a parallel event occurred on the same day in Topeka, Kansas. The Rev. Charles Parham prayed with Agnes Ozman to be baptized in the Holy Spirit. This event is generally thought to be the origin of the Pentecostal movement. From the Topeka experience came what is known as "classical Pentecostalism," but this baptism in the Holy Spirit was controversial. Many who received it were not welcome within mainline Protestant churches. Instead, they had to start denominations of their own. By the mid-1950s, this reaction began to change, and mainline churches welcomed those who had been baptized in the Holy Spirit.

The enthusiasm of Pope Leo XIII for a new outpouring of the Holy Spirit was taken over at mid-century by Pope John XXIII, who convoked the Second Vatican Council. In 1967, soon after the Council concluded, the Catholic Charismatic Renewal began. Some think the Pope's prayers for a new Pentecost were being answered. An event, now commonly known as the Duquesne Weekend, took place at the Ark and Dove Retreat House outside Pittsburgh on February 17–19, 1967. A group of college students from Duquesne University received an outpouring of the Holy Spirit, together with many charismatic gifts, like those mentioned in 1 Corinthians 12:14. One of the students was Patti Gallagher Mansfield. She and her husband Al later became leaders in the Catholic Charismatic Renewal in Louisiana.[1]

GEORGE FOX AND THE SOCIETY OF FRIENDS

The Quakers exemplify group mysticism as well. George Fox (1624–1691), the founder and most prominent leader of this movement (The Religious Society of Friends), was born and raised in the turmoil of seventeenth-century Puritan England. Fox was a bold and passionate man who acted with the assurance of knowing God firsthand. He called thousands to a direct, intimate knowledge of Christ who was present to teach and empower them. Fox's style was confrontational. For his witness he was often thrown into prison. Fox's *Journal,* in which he describes his early experience of contacts with God, or "openings," is the first in a long line of religious journals, *The Journal of John Wesley* and *The Journal of John Woolman* being among the better known. Fox's prophetic ministry led to the formation of intense prayer communities, focused on experiencing the presence of God among the people.

Richard Foster interprets the Quaker beginnings as follows:

> We have a tendency to think that, outside of the early church, true prophetic ministry is unique to us, with the early twentieth-century Pentecostal explosion or the slightly more refined charismatic renewal which broke out at mid-century in mainline churches. Basically this reflects historical ignorance combined with a touch of modern arrogance. Prophetic ministry has been going on all through the history of the Church in both healthy and unhealthy ways. Studying these . . . 'openings' of George Fox can yield useful insights into a more biblical and healthy form of prophetic witness.[2]

An Oceanic Experience

The power of the Spirit among the first Quakers produced what we today might call "an oceanic experience." Notice how George Fox uses both "sea" and "ocean" to describe his openings.

"The Lord shewed me that the natures of those things which were hurtful without were within, in the hearts and minds of wicked men. . . . The natures of these I saw within, though people had been looking without. And I cried to the Lord, saying, "Why should I be thus, seeing I was never addicted to commit those evils?" And the Lord answered that it was needful I should have a sense of all conditions, how else should I speak to all conditions; and in this I saw the infinite love of God. I also saw that there was an ocean of darkness and death, but an infinite ocean of light and love, which flowed over the ocean of darkness. And in that also I saw the infinite love of God, and I had great openings.

> And on a certain time, as I was walking in the fields, the Lord said unto me, "Thy name is written in the Lamb's book of life, which was before the foundation of the world;" and as the Lord spoke it I believed, and saw it in the new birth. Then, some time after, the Lord commanded me to go abroad into the world, which was like a briery, thorny wilderness, and when I came in the Lord's mighty power with the word of life into the world, the world swelled and made a noise like the great raging waves of the sea. Priests and professors, magistrates and people, were all like a sea, when I came to proclaim the day of the Lord amongst them and to preach repentance to them.[3]

GEORGE FOX'S POWER TO HEAL

Today it is often supposed by educated and enlightened persons that the power to cast out demons which was exercised by the early Christians has faded from the churches. An account from George Fox's *Journal* suggests otherwise. He relates how, after he was freed from Nottingham jail, he began to travel around the country, and came upon a distracted woman with her hair loose around her ears. She was being treated by a doctor, and held bound so that he could draw blood from her. Many by-standers were helping to hold her still.

Fox urged them to set her free and leave her alone, so that he could work with her spiritually. He perceived her to be spiritually tormented, and he spoke with her until she became quiet.

Fox effected a healing and quietening of her spirit. In his words: "The Lord's power settled her mind, and she mended. Afterwards she received the truth, and continued in it to her death; and the Lord's name was honoured."

Fox saw the hand of God in her healing and in many other events. "Many great and wonderful things were wrought by the heavenly power in those days; for the Lord made bare His omnipotent arm, and manifested His power, to the astonishment of many, by the healing virtue whereby many have been delivered from great infirmities. And the devils were made subject through His name; of which particular instances might be given, beyond what this unbelieving age is able to receive or bear."[4]

Richard Foster points out how many of Fox's prophetic openings were tied to ethical and moral sensibilities, a full-scale call to righteous living. Fox was actually standing in the tradition of Isaiah and Jeremiah and Amos. Fox also applied the message to himself. When he heard a voice saying, "There is one, even Christ Jesus, that can speak to thy condition," he heard this as a call to holy obedience and discipleship.

The prophetic witness is not principally focused on foretelling future events. There was an element of this in Fox's preaching, but he always put the emphasis on proclaiming the good news of the kingdom of God and calling people to conversion and lives of holiness. Further, Fox's prophetic ministry plunged him into a personal struggle. Finally, his openings resulted in a call to mission. Following his vision on Pendle Hill of a "great people to be gathered" Fox launched into extensive preaching and teaching missions. One of these was on Firbank Fell, on top of a rock which still is known as "Fox's Pulpit." A thousand people gathered around Fox as he preached for three hours. . . . Foster summarizes: "Consider also the tender ministry Fox gave to the distraught woman and how God 'settled her mind, and she mended.'"[5]

QUAKER INWARDNESS AND SILENCE

One of the most distinctive things about Quaker worship from its earliest days was the absence of any formal sacraments or ritual. Quaker worship is democratic, egalitarian, spontaneous, with men and women taking part as peers. The Quakers set aside the usual forms of liturgical Christian practice, including baptism with water and the consecration of the eucharist. In the original Quaker practice, no leaders were appointed. No formal ministers were called. Quaker meeting houses were simple places, unadorned with images or objects. Silence is the distinctive feature of Quaker worship. Out of the prevailing silence individuals–men and women–waited for the movement of the Spirit and prayed as they felt led to do. From this style of simple, common worship a kind of corporate mysticism emerged. The presence of God was, and is, keenly felt as circles gather for worship in the Quaker style.

An account of the power of Quaker group spirituality appears in a book by contemporary scientists attempting to bridge the chasm between scientific theory and faith. John Marks Templeton and Kenneth Seeman Giniger have edited *Spiritual Evolution: Scientists Discuss Their Beliefs.*[6] Ten scientists in the areas of astronomy, biology, chemistry, genetics, medicine, physics and zoology, from Australia, England, Germany, and the United States are represented. These are personal coming-to-faith essays in the great tradition of spiritual memoir, citing childhood experiences, parental influence, reading, mentors, critical faith-passages. Contributors include (among others) Peter Hodgson, Arthur Peacocke, and John Polkinghorne. Of particular interest (on the subject of group mysticism) is S. Jocelyn Bell Burnell, who is both a Quaker woman and an astronomer. Surprised by the statements of Soviets who assured her that they had not found God in outer space, Burnell expresses concerns about literalism and the old picture imagery in religious instruction. More importantly, she describes the experience of God in the gathered community: "The form of Quaker Meeting for Worship that I am used to is a community gathered in expectant silence, open, faithfully waiting for the 'promptings of love and truth' which are felt to be leadings of God. It doesn't happen every time, but there can be profound moments. . . . when the meeting collectively becomes deep, gathered, still. The presence of God may be so strongly felt that breathing is prayer and worship and communion. . . . There is a timelessness about it. . . . questions which only an hour ago seemed very important drop away as irrelevant. This present, this presence is the reality." By her knowledge *(scientia)* Burnell authenticates the Spirit. And she admits vulnerability in saying that we are neither omnipotent nor lords of the universe. Surely, this is spiritual evolution; she calls it heady stuff.

WHO WERE THE SHAKERS?
HOW DO THEY RELATE TO THE QUAKERS?

The Shakers (Society of Believers in Christ's Second Appearing) were essentially a charismatic group, a celibate millennial sect that established socialist communities in America. Dedicated to productive labor as well as a life of perfection, Shaker communities flourished economically and contributed a distinctive style of furniture, architecture and handicrafts to American culture.

They were originally derived from radical Quaker sects in England, who had adopted (from a charismatic Protestant movement known as the Camisards) certain religious practices of shaking, shouting, dancing, whirling, and speaking in tongues. Who were the Camisards? They were early eighteenth-century Protestant zealots, largely uneducated, who revolted against the government of Louis XIV. They were ecstatics who believed in prophecy and the imminent end of the world.

The Shaker doctrine, as it became known in America, was formulated by Mother Ann Lee, an illiterate textile worker of Manchester, England, who was converted to the Shaking Quakers in 1758. After experiencing persecution and imprisonment, Mother Ann had a series of revelations, after which she regarded herself—and was so regarded by her followers—as the female aspect of God's dual nature and the second incarnation of Christ. She established celibacy as the guiding principle of the sect.

Mother Ann and her followers came to America in 1774 (there were eight disciples). Their numbers grew. After Mother Ann's death in 1784, new leadership worked out the distinctive patterns of Shaker community life. Eighteen Shaker villages were established by 1826. They were located in the northeast, principally in New York State, New England and Ohio. At their height they had six thousand members, and became known for their model farms and many inventions useful in farm work, including the screw propeller, a rotary harrow, an automatic spring, a turbine waterwheel, a threshing machine, a circular saw, and the common clothespin. They were the first to package and market seeds and were once the largest producers of medicinal herbs.

Shakers were pacifists and socialists (in the sense of having commonly owned property). Spiritually, they are perhaps best known for their songs and dances, as well as for the beauty and craftsmanship of their architecture and furniture.

The number of Shakers declined so that there were just 1000 left in 1905, and only a few elderly survivors in the 1960s. Shaker life is a beautiful memory.

Many people would regard such sects as models of simplicity, like those other still surviving groups, the Mennonites and the Amish, who adopt distinctive styles of dress and more primitive ways of living. They also represent a collective mystical consciousness because of their dedication to common, sometimes charismatic prayer.

In a film called "Witness," Harrison Ford portrays a big-city cop, who becomes involved with such a simple community of believers. In the film, an Amish child has been a witness to a murder. In order to protect him, the Harrison Ford character becomes a fugitive and hides out with the Amish community. Their biblical values and behavior, including their refusal to do violence, stand in sharp contrast to the worldliness portrayed by Ford's character. Although I'm sure the film-makers didn't fully intend this, the film provides many lessons in biblical belief leading to simplicity and virtuous living.

SHAKER, QUAKER, AND CATHOLIC MYSTICISM: CONNECTIONS

Of course, Catholics are not strangers to the notion that some religious movements, especially religious orders and intentional communities, bear witness to gospel values in radical ways. Such communities develop very distinctive, Spirit-filled styles of worship. While intentional communities may take up certain kinds of austerity, they do so for a motive of celebration, in order to manifest the joy of the kingdom to the world and to each other.

Evelyn Underhill sees definite parallels between Quaker and Catholic spirituality, especially in the area of the mystical life. After reading the firsthand accounts of Quaker faith and life, based on loving surrender and the "practice of the Presence of God," Underhill sees a resemblance between their fundamental ideas and those of the French saints of roughly the same period. "At many points," she states, "the Quaker and the Catholic contemplatives approach one another."

Quaker spirituality of the second generation, in her view, was nourished not only by Jacob Boehme but also by such masters of traditional mysticism as Thomas à Kempis and Francois Fenelon. In them the Friends found principles for their religious practice and forged a link with historic Christian spirituality. Such writers influenced John Woolman (1720–1772) whose mystical awareness of the love of God brought him to denounce slavery. Woolman also developed a nearly Franciscan tenderness towards the animal creation ("the brute creatures"). Increasing maturity of soul led him to practice austerities and to take on the sorrows of the world.

The inward and active light of true Quaker spirituality passed from Woolman to a succession of strong and holy souls. Among them were: Stephen Grellet (1773–1855) and the prison reformer Elizabeth Fry (1780–1845). Underhill calls Fry "heroic." All these strong-souled Quakers partook of the same intense spirituality that had moved George Fox and his community to do remarkable deeds of holiness.

So (following Underhill) we may see the Quakers, the Shakers, and the Roman Catholic mystics as somehow linked, or at least parallel movements. All three groups are bent upon discovering an interior simplicity that comes from eyes fixed on the heart of God.

We should not be surprised that Richard Foster (who is a Quaker) quotes Francois Fenelon on simplicity: "When we are truly in this interior simplicity our whole appearance is franker, more natural. This true simplicity makes us conscious of a certain openness, gentleness, innocence, gaiety, and serenity, which is charming when we see it near to and continually, with pure eyes. Oh, how amiable this simplicity is! Who will give it to me? I leave all for this. It is the Pearl of the Gospel."[7]

JOHN WESLEY'S EVANGELICAL REVIVAL

There is no question that the intense preaching and ministry of John and Charles Wesley and their evangelical revival were a powerful influence in English and American Christianity. Wesleyan spirituality is group spirituality, but can one call it mystical?

John Wesley (1703–1791) certainly read some mystics as part of his own religious quest. Yet at a given point he disclaimed mysticism as works-righteousness and spoke against it. What was Wesley's difficulty? He thought the mystics (at least those he had read) did not sufficiently emphasize sin and repentance, but relied too much on the notions of love and self-discipline. He particularly veered away from the notion of "mystical darkness" and "the dark night of the soul."[8] It seems likely to me that if Wesley had been more broadly read in the mystics, and had understood the ways of "darkness" and "light" as alternative ways, his difficulties might not have arisen. Teresa of Avila writes extensively about sin, as does John of the Cross, but John Wesley did not read either. However, it seems likely that post-Reformation difficulties were also at work.

Yet John Wesley was deeply versed in some mystical writers, whom he later included in the Christian library he edited: a collection of abridgements of the great Christian classics. Among the Christian mystics who appeared in Wesley's Christian library were: Macarius, Francois Fenelon, Blaise Pascal, Brother Lawrence, John of Avila, Gregory Lopez, Madame Bourignon, and Molinos. De Renty and Madame Guyon[9] were published separately.

Robert G. Tuttle, Jr., an authority on Wesley's life and thought, suggests that Wesley embraced important aspects of the devotional thought of many Christian mystics but avoided their language. "Most of the basic characteristics of Wesley's doctrine find parallel consideration among those mystics whom he was reading while his ideas on perfection were first being formulated. The following statement by Wesley concerning the implications of Christian perfection could just as easily been written by any of the Roman Catholic mystics already discussed: Perfection is loving God with all the heart, so that every evil temper is destroyed; and every thought and word and work springs from and is conducted to the end by pure love of God and our neighbor."[10] In the end, Wesley came to advocate (it is Tuttle's term) a "mysticism of service." Tuttle suggests that an early influence towards such a "mysticism of service" may have come from an early reading the life of Ignatius of Loyola (John Wesley read it on August 16, 1742.) While Loyola was not one of the mystics he most admired, he included John of Avila in his Christian library, John of Avila (who had been a counselor to his kinswoman, Teresa of Avila) was in turn deeply influenced by Loyola.

Another authority on the Wesleys, Frank Whaling, holds that ". . . the notion that Wesley suddenly repudiated the mystical influences on his development and abandoned them forever is an erroneous one, just as erroneous as the notion that because he was suspicious of the antinomian tendencies he saw in Luther and Calvin that he therefore abandoned those reformers. He assimilated the things that were helpful to him, and to the movement that grew up as a result of his work, from any and every source."[11] Whaling goes on to observe that the mystical writers (in Wesley's Christian Library and all the mystics he read, including the Church Fathers) "played their part in Wesley's reconciliation of the seemingly opposed notions of justification, sanctification, and Christian perfection." Most of all, Whaling reminds us, John Wesley's concern was not for Christian scholarship or doctrinal debate but for a lived spirituality that would draw on the best of past and present.

THOMAS MERTON AND THE SHAKERS

It seems likely that the greatest factor in group mysticism and group spirituality is its expression of joy: joy in the knowledge of one's own salvation and nearness to God. Consider Thomas Merton's attraction to both Quakers and Shakers. In his early quest for faith, and later, when he was already in a Cistercian monastery, Merton was deeply attracted by both groups.

Merton's mother was a Quaker. Merton himself attended Quaker meetings in his own pursuit of God. That is detailed in his own conversion story, *The Seven Storey Mountain*.[12] He was mildly attracted to Quaker practice, especially silent prayer, but he wanted more, the more that he eventually found in Catholic life and practice.

A recently published work by Thomas Merton is called *Seeking Paradise: The Spirit of the Shakers*. It contains photographs of Shaker buildings and furniture taken by Thomas Merton himself and by Paul M. Pearson, the writer-photographer who assembled this book. Essentially, Pearson is attempting to discover what drew Merton to the Shakers; what parallels he may have found between Cistercian life and Shaker life. It all seems to come back to simplicity, beauty, and joy.

Pearson says: "The essential Shaker message was deeply Christian. Unlike many Puritan sects they were not 'men of a dour, sulphur and brimstone eschatology,' but, as Merton writes, 'simple, joyous, optimistic people whose joy was rooted in the fact that Christ had come, and that the basic Christian experience was the discovery of Christ living in all of us now. . . .' Believing in 'a redeemed cosmos in which war, hatred, tyranny and greed have no place–a cosmos of creativity and worship.'"

Merton's basic insights about the Shakers are:

First, the Shakers are seeking paradise. They are longing for a return to primal innocence, the so-called 'Original blessing' and that longing for a return to Eden brings beauty and simplicity to everything they do and make. He sees, for instance, in Shaker barns a "highly mystical quality," a certain unearthly light: capaciousness, dignity, solidity, and permanence.

Second, they believe in the sacredness of work. Each item that the craftsman makes participates in God's work of creation. Merton speaks of "desiring the good of the work," "desiring the inner truth of the work," and "the conscience of the worker," namely a conscience so formed that he will think only of the good and truth of the work, and will avoid anything shoddy. The Shaker craftsman has an ideal—to make every object fulfill its vocation. "In both their work and their worship," Merton says, the Shakers attempted to be "attuned to the music intoned in each being by God the Creator and by the Lord Jesus."

A third insight, which stems from the Shakers, but is by no means exclusive to them, has something to do with joy. Merton wrote powerfully about the dance of creation. At the time of his keenest interest in the Shakers, he was revising his book, *Seeds of Contemplation*. The new chapter he added was called "The General Dance."

Merton was corresponding with Edward Deming Andrews (curator of the Shaker community at Pleasant Hill) and told him of his discovery of an old Christmas carol "about the dancing of God with man in the mystery of the Incarnation. The opening words of this carol are: "Tomorrow shall be my dancing day. . . ."

The carol tells the story of Christ from his Incarnation through his Ascension.

> Then up to Heaven did I ascend
> Where now I dwell in sure substance
> On the right hand of God that man
> May come unto the general dance.

Merton took this discovery of a dancing God into his new chapter for *New Seeds of Contemplation*.

The Lord plays and diverts himself in the garden of his creation, and if we could go out of our own obsession with what we think is the meaning of it all, we might be able to hear his call. . . .

For the world and time are the dance of the Lord in emptiness. The silence of the spheres is the music of a wedding feast. . . . no despair of ours can alter the reality of things, or strain the joy of the cosmic dance which is always there. Indeed, we are in the midst of it, and it is in the midst of us, for it beats in our blood, whether we want it to or not.

Yet the fact remains that we are invited to forget ourselves on purpose, cast our awful solemnity to the winds, and join in the general dance.

Pearson ends with these words by Thomas Merton: "Merton invites us, as he wrote in a 1964 message to Latin American poets, to 'Come, dervishes: here is the water of life. Dance in it.'"[13]

DERVISHES: THOSE DANCING MYSTICS

Who, then, are the dervishes to whom Merton refers, and what do they have to teach contemporary people? Dervishes are mystics; they exemplify group mysticism; and they belong to one of the Islamic mystical orders who practice poverty and live in secluded quarters, or who roam about as pious beggars. The word *dervish,* comes from a Persian word meaning "beggar;" that is, one who stands at the *dar* or city gate. In Arabic countries a dervish is called a *faquir,* that is, a poor man, or *sufi.* Sufi mysticism is world-renowned and respected. Rumi, the Iranian scholar and poet (Jalal al-Dn al-Rumi 1207–1273), is thought to be the founder of Sufi mysticism, the tradition to which the dervishes belong. Some of the dervishes use prolonged repetition of bodily movements. They move in unison, shouting out religious sayings, in order to enter into trances or ecstasies. Therefore they are commonly called "whirling dervishes" or sometimes "dancing" or "howling dervishes."[14]

So we have seen that mysticism may develop a special intensity in communities and groups. Sometimes the mystical consciousness of one person is taken up by an entire group, and preserves its distinctive character from generation to generation. Sometimes a single person stands out as representing the group's spirit—George Fox, perhaps, or Thomas Merton. Yet there is also a hidden mysticism which prevails in the middle of everyday, ordinary existence. What is it like, and even if it is not showy or remarkable, can we describe it nevertheless?

CHAPTER TWELVE

A Mysticism of
Everyday Life

n 1990 a delegation of American Jews—
some of whom had been involved in
Buddhist meditation—went to visit the
Dalai Lama and his assemblage of Tibetan
Buddhist monks. The meetings took place
in India, and were captured in prose by the
American writer Rodger Kamenetz in his
book, *The Jew in the Lotus: A Poet's Rediscovery of Jewish
Identity in Buddhist India.*

There were many aspects to this dialogue, which focused on
questions which the Tibetans wanted to pose about Judaism.
In particular, they wanted to know how a religion could be
long maintained without a homeland. A further passionate
interest expressed by the Dalai Lama was to understand
Jewish mysticism. After much hemming and hawing by the

group, the American, Rabbi Zalman Schachter, took the lead in explaining Jewish mysticism.

"Our teachings (i.e., mystical teachings) have been kept secret even from Jews for a long time. So every day, when people get up and say their prayers, there is an exoteric order. But hidden inside the exoteric is the esoteric, the deep attunement, the deep way."[1]

This deep way is the way of the *kabbalah* which means "tradition" or "what has been received." The *kabbalah* claims an ancient origin has been passed down through an oral tradition from master to student, and draws inspiration both from canonical and later texts. Canonical texts include Genesis, The Song of Songs, and Ezekiel. Later written literature includes *Sefer Yetzirah (The Book of Formation)* and *Zohar, or the Book of Splendor.*

Rabbi Schachter had already grasped the spiritual goal of Tibetan Buddhist teaching: a fundamental orientation toward the nature, cause, and elimination of suffering. The Buddhist path toward personal transformation leads through a series of systematic meditations. The goal is to become a compassionate person, a living buddha, who will help to free others from the suffering of human existence.

Jewish mysticism takes a very different view, Schachter began to explain, through a complete cosmology, based on a mystical interpretation of Genesis. Kabbalists find in Genesis the creation of not one but four worlds, corresponding to the four letters of the name of God, *yod, he, vov,* and *he* (which transliterated into English is "Yahweh," the name of God that Jews do not pronounce out loud). These four worlds are correlated by Jewish mystics to the elements of earth, air, water, and fire.

As he listened, Kamenetz (who had been invited along as a devout Jew who could write about the Buddhist-Jewish exchange) began to understand Schachter's explanation. This four-worlds cosmology, he realized, came straight out of the

Lurianic *kabbalah*, as received from the early Hasidic masters and finally formulated by the Chabad Hasidim and the late eighteenth-century rabbi who founded the Lubavitch sect.[2]

". . . In the Hasidic tradition, when one *davens* (prays) with true *kavannah* (intention) the four worlds of body, heart, mind and spirit are called upon. Specific meditations are used to connect the words of a given prayer to the *sefirot*. What are the *sefirot*? While the word literally means "numbers," its larger meaning is "the supernal lights, divine aspects, grades and attributes of God." The seven lower *sefirot* are given in 1 Chronicles 29:11.[3] "Through prayer," Kamenetz explains, "recited with inward intention, one rises from world to world to reach the goal of nearness to God."[4]

Kamenetz, who has now become a leader in the American Jewish renewal movement, suggests that this mystical element underlies all of Jewish prayer, but its fundamentals and even the existence of a mystical realm are not understood by most practicing Jews. In the dialogue with the Dalai Lama, Rabbi Schachter was surfacing aspects of Judaism which the other Jewish teachers on the team hardly knew about, or would not seek to emphasize.

Rabbi Schachter had prepared himself deeply for this dialogue with the Buddhists before embarking on the journey. "I was aware that inside of me there was a movement preparing for this event. All my reading, dreaming, talking with students and friends, praying and meditation . . ." were what Schachter called "getting there in *kavannah* before actually arriving" in Dharamsala. *Kavannah* does not only mean "intention," it also means a group of structured intentional practices meant to lend greater depth and force to one's ordinary prayer.[5] In short, Schachter was well prepared and deeply qualified to speak to the Buddhists about Jewish mystical life.

A startling aspect of Jewish mysticism arose when Rabbi Schachter attempted to explain to the Buddhists about angels.

In an effort to communicate, Schachter had used the Buddhist expression *deva*, which means a minor divinity or deity. Buddhists do not believe in a single creator deity, but they do believe in minor divinities, higher beings called *devas* whose nature is not fully understood. Some Buddhists regard them as mental projections.

The mention of angels by the Jewish rabbi set off a flurry of eager questions from the Dalai Lama and his associates. Schachter began to explain the massive power of angelic beings—the idea that each group or nation has its own protective angel, that the realms of angels are vast and numerous, that even the dark angels (Satan being chief among them) are part of God's plan and subject to God's sovereignty.

It is striking that Kamenetz, a revivalist contemporary Jew, consistently refers to Jewish mystical knowledge as esoteric, and sees a danger that this knowledge of deep and prayerful contact with God is in danger of being lost to the present generation. From his account one can easily speculate that the strong interest by some Jews in Buddhist meditation is an effort to recover the lost mystical attributes of their own Jewish faith.

A second teacher of mysticism among the group of delegates was Rabbi Jonathan Omer-Man, who warned his fellow Jews that he was going to be "more extreme than Zalman and I don't want to be told that I'm not in the mainstream." The early Talmudists, Rabbi Omer-Man explained, constituted a mystical elite. Their experience had been passed down through Hasidism "which made it simpler and helped bring 'the esoteric to ordinary Jews everywhere.'" Omer-Man lamented that this esoteric tradition is not available to seekers within their own synagogues when certain rabbis are either unaware of it or not interested. Incidentally, Kamenetz agrees that this is true. Most rabbis haven't studied *kabbalah* and, with their other commitments to youth programs and social services and the outward life of the synagogue, wouldn't have time to do so. But Omer-Man believes that this esoteric prayer of the heart is what is undergirding all of Jewish prayer.

In response to questions from the Buddhists, Rabbi Omer-Man attempted to describe Jewish meditation, discerning two basic types: "One attempts to open a person up to greater insight, clarity and vision. The other works on 'purifying the vessel, changing the human being, making the human being more perfect.'" To a certain extent, Kamenetz says, these two distinct forms of meditation have purposes that overlap.[6]

The first type of meditation, which is done during prayer, involves focusing on sounds and chanting. The name of God is chanted by using the different consonants *yod, he, vov*, and *he*, which make up the name of God although this is not pronounced aloud in Judaism. By connecting these consonants with various vowel sounds, chants are created which connect to different aspects of the body. Jonathan Omer-Man described this kind of meditation as influencing "different parts of who we are, different powers in different names." By this meditation, connections are being made with the ten aspects of God given in the *sefirot*: (1) *Keter* (Crown), (2) *Chochmah* (Wisdom), (3) *Binah* (Understanding), (4) *Chesed* (Kindness), (5) *Gevurah* (Power), (6) *Tifert* (Beauty), (7) *Netzach* (Endurance), (8) *Hod* (Majesty), (9) *Yesod* (Foundation), and (10) *Malhkhut* (Kingdom). Through meditation and prayer one approaches God through these ten aspects of his divinity.

The second type of Jewish meditation aims at transformation of the personality, but it is very different from the Buddhist meditation although it has a similar goal. This second type of Jewish meditation is closer to what Christians might call "spiritual exercises." They may often occur in dialogue with a spiritual master or teacher, and can rely on storytelling,

139

especially the stories handed down by the Hasidic masters. All
these stories contain pearls of embedded spiritual and moral
wisdom. The spiritual candidates may engage in other spiritual
disciplines as well. One, for instance, is the so-called path of
joy, in which the seeker works, through laughter, singing, and
wine-drinking, to enter a level of celebration. A second is the path
of tears—tears shed not for personal losses, but for the sorrows of
the Jewish people, for the pain of exile, and for the brokenness of
the world. A third meditation consists of crying out loudly to
God, expressing fear, loneliness, and one's need for God's care.

Kamenetz emphasizes that Jewish mysticism is a mysticism
of this world. Judaism has had (with the possible exception of
the Essenes) no expressions of monasticism, and the temple
priesthood is only a memory. Judaism is practiced in the
world, in the midst of family life and civic commitment. Even
when Hasidic communities form, alight with zeal and flushed
with messianic yearning, they nevertheless are firmly located
within (mostly) metropolitan life: as in the Williamsburg section
of Brooklyn. Moreover, Jewish spirituality expresses a yearning
for the presence of God in our midst (*Shekinah*) and for
Tikkun Olan, "the repair of the world."

A Mysticism of Joy in the World

Karl Rahner (1905–1984), a major twentieth-century theologian and one of the chief architects of Vatican II, has written about a mysticism of delight in the world. Rahner, who
became a Jesuit in 1922, was ordained in 1932 and earned his
doctorate under Martin Honecker 1936. During World War II
he taught and did pastoral work in Vienna. After the war he
held professorships of dogmatic theology at the Universities of
Innsbruck, Munich, and Munster.

Rahner was a prolific writer and editor. His *Theological
Investigations* alone includes fourteen volumes. He wrote

more than three thousand published articles. Rahner's thought (and participation) influenced much of the language and content of the documents of Vatican II. His vision was world-embracing, and provided theological support for openness and dialogue between Catholics and other Christians, as well as a recognition of God's love for all humankind.

Rahner was also a man of intense spirituality. Looking over the tremendous productivity of his life, it is easy to see Rahner as one who practices a spirituality of the world. He himself was a man of deep prayer, but in no way would he be willing to appropriate the title of mystic. Yet he believed that mystical prayer could be practiced within an ordinary schedule as part of a busy life focused on practical achievement.

In response to a request, Rahner wrote and delivered a paper on the theme, "An Ignatian Mysticism of Joy in the World," which later became a chapter in his collected *Theological Investigations.*[7] In it he wrestled with the apparent conflict between loving God in the world—seeing the presence of God in the world, and the monk's call (or the Jesuit's call) to forsake the world and live entirely in the service of Jesus Christ. Are these two calls really in opposition, or do they merely seem so? Rahner uses the historic term *fuga saeculi*, a flight from the age, that is to say, the world of one's own generation and time, as one pole of the argument. At the other pole is a mysticism of the world. "The basis of flight from the world," he writes, "constitutes the intrinsic possibility of Ignatian acceptance of the world." The first assertion he makes about Ignatian piety is that it embraces the foolishness of the Cross. His second fundamental assertion is that Ignatian piety is directed towards the God who is beyond the whole world and yet freely reveals himself in the world, to us who are in the world.

Rahner is a rare bird among theologians because he takes mysticism seriously as a source for theological reflection. The great mystics present us with a paradigm of faith, hope, and love. They illuminate for us what is happening in the lives of all persons of genuine faith. Rahner affirms that mysticism may be present and active even when a full-blown mystical theology is lacking. When people don't know what mysticism is, when theologians have failed to explain it to them, nevertheless there may be a mystical dimension in faith, life and prayer, even among the most ordinary persons.

Karl Rahner and his brother Hugo, also a distinguished Jesuit scholar, reflect this incarnational spirituality in occasional prayers they wrote for their brother Jesuits. Hugo Rahner writes: "Lord Jesus Christ . . . you yourself are here, our beloved simple bread. In the midst of our ordinary daily routine you are here. You are here in the marketplace of everyday life, amid the wretched and the labored course of our earthly hours and in the busy flight of the weeks and years. Be then the bread of my daily life. Be the deepest meaning of my study and work. . . ."[8]

ORDINARY PERSONS SEEKING HOLINESS

When I first took up the spiritual life in earnest I was living in the Borough of Queens in New York City. I began to attend Mass daily, or almost daily, on weekdays, at a nearby church, Our Lady Queen of Martyrs. There, at seven AM, often before daylight and in the coldest weather, a small crowd of mostly older people gathered to participate in Holy Eucharist, some with their rosaries held reverently in their hands. The Mass lasted less than a half-hour each day. The large, darkened church was empty, except for these few faithful souls. Yet, over time, as I attended this service, I became conscious of transformation: the on-going development of holiness among this small band of faithful Roman Catholic Christians. No doubt my own zeal was lighting up the place—I had somehow just discovered the spiritual life. The word "mystic" was not constantly on my lips or anyone else's; but I began to observe how grace was working in the fidelity of these ordinary lives.

There was another group in that same church that taught me similar lessons about the work of grace in ordinary lives. At that time the Roman Catholic Church established for the first time "extraordinary ministers of the Eucharist": lay people who were officially appointed to give communion in the absence of "ordinary" ministers, the priests and deacons who were the usual distributors of the consecrated wafers. My husband and I were among the first lay group in that parish who were so designated. Our task was to take holy communion to shut-ins in their apartments near the church, as well as to elderly people confined to neighboring nursing homes. In this way I went with another woman minister to distribute communion to some thirty persons on a Sunday in a nearby nursing home. This practice was changing us for the better; it was changing our communicants too.

I came to understand the deep devotion underlying many Catholic customs which had long been strange to me. One of these was the practice on the part of the faithful of reverencing or kissing the hands of a priest, especially a newly ordained priest. Myself a convert to Roman Catholic faith, I had accepted many Catholic beliefs but not all of Catholic practice. Imagine my astonishment when, on a given Sunday morning, a woman communicant, having received communion from me, began to kiss my hands. She was of European origin, a Polish immigrant, I believe. I was taken aback but also moved by her gesture. I understood, perhaps for the first time, the depth of devotion experienced in a hidden way by many inarticulate members of the faithful. Since I was not a priest, I grasped at once that this devotional gesture was offered not to the priest or minister, but to Jesus Christ believed to be present in the sacrament.

Brother Lawrence, an Everyday Mystic

The notion of an everyday mysticism is well exemplified by Brother Lawrence of the Resurrection. His wise observations, as we have noted, were collected as *The Practice of the Presence of God,* which has become a spiritual classic. A lay brother, Lawrence worked in a Discalced Carmelite monastery as a cook and sandal maker.

Brother Lawrence's original name was Nicholas Herman. He was a man raised in poor circumstances and without much education. Surely, Brother Lawrence would not have expected to become a famous teacher and example of prayer, but so he is. His menial role within the Carmelite monastery in Paris excluded him from many of the more formal solemnities of the house. This exclusion (it was true for all the lay brothers) may have been a blessing in disguise. Brother Lawrence developed a habit of being in God's presence during all the ordinary activities of his day. After some early struggles to gain a footing in spiritual life, he came to regard himself as centered in God. Thus he developed a spirituality of great modesty and practicality, one which can be practiced by anyone whose days are not free for meditation and contemplation.

At first Brother Lawrence struggled with a deep sense of his own unworthiness before God. Over a lifetime he never fully overcame his low opinion of himself. When he prayed, he thought about death, judgment, hell, and paradise, as well as his own sins, a habit which left him constantly sad and weary. When these formal exercises were over, he would resort to another spiritual activity, which he called "the practice of the presence of God." In this method, Brother Lawrence remained in God's love, trustingly leaving aside monumental issues. There he began to find peace and consolation. "This gave me a great reverence for God, and in this matter faith alone was my reassurance."[9]

Essentially, Brother Lawrence developed his method by trial and error because it helped him to deal with his continual and consuming anxieties. "When I accepted the fact that I might spend my life suffering from these troubles and anxieties—which in no way diminished the trust I had in God and served only to increase my faith—I found myself changed all at once. And my soul, until that time always in turmoil, experienced a deep inner peace as if it had found its center and place of rest."

The result of this discovery—about remaining in the presence of God—brought about a real change in Brother Lawrence. First of all, he gave up all devotions and prayers that were not required and devoted himself exclusively to staying in the presence of God. This gave him an entirely new challenge, namely, a question of how to deal with his overwhelming joy and contentment. This joy couldn't be allowed to show, lest people suspect him of silliness, foolishness, or pride. Brother Lawrence had to learn how to maintain a calm demeanor in spite of the fact that he was happy most of the time. "I keep myself in his presence by simple attentiveness and a general loving awareness of God that I call 'actual presence of God' or better, a secret conversation of the soul with God that is lasting. This sometimes results in interior, or exterior contentment and joys so great that I have to perform childish acts, appearing more like folly than devotion, to control them and keep them from showing outwardly."[10]

What is the difference between the formal prayer that was causing Brother Lawrence so much anxiety and the simple restful style of prayer he came to in the end? No doubt volumes can be written about this difference. Mainly it seems to be a shift of focus that Brother Lawrence made between dwelling on his own flawed nature and dwelling instead on the over-flowing kindness and mercy of God. "By practicing the presence of God, the soul becomes so intimate with God that it spends all its life in continual acts of love, adoration, contrition, trust, thanksgiving, oblation, petition and all the most excellent virtues. Sometimes it even becomes one continuous act, because the soul constantly practices this exercise of his divine presence."[11]

Brother Lawrence says that few souls will reach this advanced state of continual contact with God. Yet by his writings he makes this continuing practice of God's presence seem much more accessible to ordinary people in everyday lives. Lawrence says that to arrive at this state, God must give us a special measure of grace. If we do not receive such graces, we can still develop a loving awareness of God that is almost like the practice of the presence of God. Lawrence is right to say that God must grant the grace. Yet his notion is that we ourselves can reach towards the grace of God by what he calls "a substituted awareness." This awareness that Brother Lawrence wants us to try for, almost but not quite like the thing itself, reveals something about his distinctive approach— his governing modesty and simplicity of heart.

ALPHONSUS RODRIGUEZ, PORTER

There are other examples of "everyday mystics," well-known and honored as such in their own times but less well-known to us. St. Alphonsus Rodriguez is one of these. Born in Segovia, Spain in 1532, he was the son of a wool merchant who was reduced to poverty. Alphonsus (in Spanish Alfonso) married at twenty-six and became a widower (with one living child) at thirty-one. Alfonso began an intense practice of the spiritual life. After his child's death he wanted to become a religious, but lacked the education. Eventually, at age forty, he became a Jesuit lay brother. Six months after entering the Society of Jesus he was assigned to the newly founded college at Majorca, where he served as a porter for forty-six years.

Not unlike Brother Lawrence (who came later) Alphonsus Rodriguez maintained a continual and recollected contact with God in the middle of very distracting menial employment. He exercised a marvelous influence on many who lived in the college, known as intellectuals, especially St. Peter Claver, who led an illustrious life as a missionary to South America. Brother Alphonsus also served as a spiritual director and counselor to many who came to see him at his porter's lodge. One reason, perhaps, that he is not so well known today is that he did not write a major spiritual treatise.[12] But, by all accounts, Brother Alfonso or Alphonsus, who died in 1617, was remarkable for his personal holiness; he was inspirational to many who knew him.

Rodriguez was declared a saint in a long process. Delays were caused by controversies, not about him, but about the Jesuits. Brother Alphonsus was first named "venerable" in 1626, just nine years after his death. He wasn't beatified until 1826, and was finally canonized in 1887. Since 1633 he has been considered the patron of the city and island of Majorca. His obscurity seems rather fitting, somehow, for he never sought fame, and belongs among the many Christians who have practiced a prayer of the ordinary life.

Brother Alphonsus was immortalized, however, in a brief poem by Gerard Manley Hopkins. In it, Hopkins says that many gain notoriety through heroic and warlike exploits, but others conduct "the war within." Rodriguez is one of these. Hopkins writes of "the brand we wield/Unseen, the heroic breast not outward-steeled."

> Yet God (that hews mountain and continent,
> Earth, all, out; who, with trickling increment,
> Veins violets and tall trees makes more and more)
> Could crowd career with conquest while there went
> Those years and years of world without event
> That in Majorca Alfonso watched the door.[13]

PRACTICAL (EVEN IF HIDDEN) MYSTICISM

Rodger Kamenetz has suggested that a hidden mystical element is vital to all Jewish prayer, even when it is unrecognized. Karl Rahner, a major Catholic theologian, speaks of a mysticism of the world as being fundamental to the Ignatian vision. Brother Lawrence of the Resurrection provides a modest and unobtrusive style of mystical prayer, called "the practice of the presence of God," which fits easily within the life of the lowliest lay brother in a French Carmelite monastery. This lowly style of prayer discovered by Brother Lawrence can be readily practiced in contemporary life.

So it seems we must add "everydayness" to the distinctive characteristics of the mystical life. Whatever its intense character, its affirmative and negative movements, its distinctive arc or progression, nevertheless the mystical life is also marked by perseverance and a kind of lowly simplicity. By such "everydayness" the mystic is able to continue and press on, knowing God inwardly, and cultivating a transforming intimacy over time. Yet, as we shall see, these mystics—whether anonymous or well-known—are able to develop a world-embracing vision. It is perhaps for this reason that mystics are sometimes seen as the elite who will lead the rest of us into a transformed future.

CHAPTER THIRTEEN

World-Transforming Mysticism

n his book, *Dancing Madly Backwards: A Journey into God,* Paul Marechal writes of a mystical vision of humanity and the world. In the preface to that book, Morton Kelsey writes: "The world is very mysterious. It is full of paradoxes and unfinished stories. Many of us try to avoid these paradoxes and finish the stories. Only a few step deliberately into this mystery, the religious way. Paul Marechal has been on this journey for many years. And now he shares that journey. . . . records his journey in stories and narratives, poetry and images. . . ."[1]

There is something of Thomas Merton's confrontation with mystery in Marechal's lovely, poetic book. Especially pertinent to the notion of a world-transforming mysticism is his chapter called "In the Heart of a Great Round Dance."

Marechal begins with Narnia, the imaginary world of C. S. Lewis's series, *The Chronicles of Narnia*. He quotes Lewis to this effect:

> "The further up and further in you go, the bigger everything gets. The inside is larger than the outside."
>
> Lucy looked hard at the garden and saw that it was not really a garden at all but a whole world, with its own rivers and woods and sea and mountains. But they were not strange: she knew them all.
>
> "I see," she said, "this is still Narnia, and more real and more beautiful than the Narnia down below. . . . I see . . .world within world, Narnia within Narnia."
>
> "Yes," said Mr. Tumnus, "like an onion: except that as you continue to go in and in, each circle is larger than the last."[2]

From this point of departure Marechal, a lifelong contemplative, offers a broad and deep interpretation. "Trees and people have this much in common. Each is an ecstasy of depth within depth, world within world, Narnia within Narnia."

Like Lewis and others, Marechal must resort to stories and pictures in order to convey what I have called *transparency*, the heightened vision or deeper grasp of reality that comes about from a sustained experience of prayer. To the person of prayer and spiritual dwelling with God, everything in the universe discloses a deeper and larger meaning. Marechal suggests that by a resort to silence and reflection, soundlessness and meditation, we can enter into the realm that science has yet to understand— the force that unifies everything.

> If we could see . . . we would see into layers of depth: molecular, atomic, subatomic . . . we would see those levels melt into depth, and into the silence of infinity. . . .
>
> If we could see, we would see what the philosophers call 'being': an intimate depth shared by every pocket of creation. We would experience the level where—according to Bell's theorem—everything is connected. Today physicists are

finding that some unknown force, traveling faster than the speed of light, ties everything together. But to see this force field we have to tiptoe quietly down long flights of stairs, to the 'level' where music is flowing out of unseen strings. We have to settle down into the kernel of the tree, where Narnia transcends Narnia.

It is at this level of depth and insight, one which we arrive at by descending mystical "long flights of stairs," that Marechal says we will find truth.

We will see total truth, the fragrance of apparently divergent 'worlds' intersecting to become the temple of the Great Round Dance.[3]

Where does this phrase, "The Great Round Dance," come from? Why, from the Greek Fathers, Marechal explains. "The Greek Fathers describe the Trinity as a Great Round Dance in which Love flames forth from one Person to the Other in a flow that never ceases. Its deep melody carries on night and day. . . ."

It was through this book that I came to know Paul Marechal again. We were in our forties, but remembered that we had become friends at age ten or eleven, because we were neighbors in New Orleans. In the early 1980s I found him again as the author of this profound mystical book, then a layman and a schoolteacher in Covington, Louisiana, on the north shore of Lake Pontchartrain. Marechal had already been a monk and a teacher of prayer. He had left the monastery, but wanted to return. He did so, and became known as Brother Elias at the Cistercian monastery in Conyers, Georgia.

Brother Elias himself, and his book, *Dancing Madly Backwards*, remind me that contemplatives and mystics have a profound message to bring to the rest of us, one that they must express in comparisons and metaphors.

The world is deeply connected within the Divine Reality. The God who as Creator is beyond all things is also present to us within all things when we are willing to become conscious of that presence.

Because mystical writers are so sensitive to the depth of the world (worlds within worlds) and the presence of God in the world, it is tempting to anoint them as an elite who can lead the rest of us toward a less hostile and more peaceful worldwide civilization. As impractical as this idea sounds, it has a kind of hopefulness about it.

During the 1960s in the United States the idea of consciousness-raising took hold, principally as a political tool. Groups calling themselves consciousness-raising groups were formed to come to grips with injustices within society. In particular, this method became a part of the women's movement.

At that time my heart turned in another direction. Influenced by the rich intellectual and social climate of New York City, where I was then living, I seized upon the idea of transformation of consciousness as a tool for changing the world. Immediately I came to understand that the spiritual life begins not with transforming another person's consciousness but through transformation of one's own consciousness. For the Christian, this profound change—conversion and sanctification—is rooted in the life of grace.

Contemporary Catholic theologians—Karl Rahner is one of them—were beginning to resist the idea that grace is a scattered and random affair. We do not live in a universe in which pockets of goodness may burst upon us rarely in the middle of a gray and alienated world. No. A new vision was coming about, through Karl Rahner and many others, to suggest that we are living in grace; that the divine initiative is everywhere seeking us out and summoning us to a transformation of ourselves and of the unjust structures that govern human behavior.

During the decade of the 1970s, when many Americans were exploring consciousness through New Age methodologies and secular "sensitivity training," at Esalen in California and elsewhere, it became clear to me that a deep mystical consciousness within Christianity had always been part of our heritage and could now be re-appropriated as part of a world-transforming spirituality.

It was a kind of unpacking of John Donne's oft-quoted sermon:

> No man is an island entire of itself; every man is a piece of the continent, a part of the main (mainland). . . . Every man's death diminishes me, because I am involved in mankind, and therefore never send to know for whom the Bell tolls: it tolls for thee.[4]

All those centuries ago, Donne, from the pulpit at St. Paul's in London, had voiced the interconnectedness of humanity. To do so, he did not need to depart from Christian orthodoxy. The connectedness of humanity seemed to him a plainly Christian idea.

Now, however, with the rapid pace of globalization a factor in all our lives, the question of what might constitute a world-embracing Christianity has taken on a different tone.

Mysticism can be found in all the major world religions and many of the minor ones. Does this mean that mysticism can cut across religions and cultures, creating a world-embracing mysticism that transcends all religions and denominations? This may in fact be the outcome of the encounter between world religions and cultures. But there is another way to look at the encounter between mystics of differing religious traditions.

When Thomas Merton was a student at Columbia, he was deeply attracted by the spiritual life. In his circle was an Indian monk, known to the group as "Bramachari." (It turns out that Bramachari was really a sort of nickname; Bramachari is an Indian word for "student"). Merton observed with amazement how Bramachari prayed, attentively, at various times of the day. More importantly, he noticed how happy it made him.

Ultimately, Merton resolved to ask him whether he should embrace the Hindu tradition to which Bramachari belonged.

Bramachari advised Merton otherwise. No, he explained to Merton, you should investigate your own history of contemplation and mystical encounter. Read St. Augustine, he counseled. When I first read this story I was amazed at the forbearance shown by the Indian, who failed to pounce on a prospective convert as he might have done. The Indian had a larger vision, in which Christianity had a place, and a role to play. Moreover, he had clearly investigated the Christian mystical tradition and knew it was worth its salt.

It is true that over a lifetime Thomas Merton, practicing silence and contemplation within the Christian tradition, nevertheless wanted to bring about some ecumenical reconciliation with the religions of the East, which during the 1960s were exercising a particular attraction to Americans. Yet Merton himself is a key figure in the revival and continuation of Christian contemplative life, which has its own richness and history.

When we want to understand how believers can come to a world-embracing vision (never more necessary than in a world being "made smaller" by technology) we must turn not only to the practice of prayer but also to the worldview of faith. In the words of Teilhard de Chardin:

> Faith, as we understand it here is not, of course, simply the intellectual adherence to Christian dogma. It is taken in a much richer sense to mean belief in God charged with all the trust in his beneficent strength that the knowledge of the divine being arouses in us. It means the practical conviction that the universe, between the hands of the Creator, still continues to be the clay in which He shapes innumerable possibilities according to His will. In a word, it is *evangelical faith*, of which it can be said that no virtue, not even charity, was more strongly urged by the Saviour.[5]

As long ago as 1926 Teilhard de Chardin was observing humanity going through a new process of growth and transformation. "What is happening under our eyes within the mass of peoples? What is the cause of this disorder in society, this uneasy agitation, these swelling waves, these whirling and mingling currents, and these turbulent and formidable new impulses?"

Teilhard, himself a scientist, was referring to many convergent forces: the rapid pace of technological growth, the multiplying knowledge coming from the sciences, remarkable technical leaps in communications, as well as the growth of world population.

Humanity, he insists, "is visibly passing through a crisis of growth. . . . becoming dimly aware of its shortcomings and its capacities." Humanity under this new kind of tension "sees the universe growing luminous like the horizon just before sunrise. It has a sense of premonition and attraction."[6]

And although he is a scientist he sees grace and prayer as actual forces in the cosmic drama: "If we want the divine *milieu* to grow all around us, then we must jealously guard all the forces of union, of desire, and of prayer that grace offers us. By the mere fact that our transparency will increase, the divine light, that never ceases to press in upon us, will irrupt the more powerfully.[7]

This power of divinization that Teilhard speaks of is God's power acting in every dimension of our universe, drawing humanity together through power and grace. "Across the immensity of time and the disconcerting multiplicity of individuals, one single operation is taking place: the annexation to Christ of his chosen; one single thing is being made: the Mystical Body of Christ, starting from all the sketchy spiritual powers scattered throughout the world." Teilhard says that each one of us is called to see God face to face; but that ultimate vision will be inseparably connected to the "elevating and illuminating action of Christ."[8]

The transforming effects of this divinization will link human beings one to another. "Our individual mystical effort awaits an essential completion in its union with the mystical effort of all other men."[9]

Teilhard is more hopeful about the advance of progress than many observers. Possibly that is because he says we are not in competition with God. "The greater man becomes, the more humanity becomes united, with consciousness of, and mastery of, its potentialities, the more beautiful creation will be, the more perfect adoration will become, and the more Christ will find, for mystical extensions, a body worthy of resurrection." I think Teilhard is here referring to all humanity as being drawn into the so-called "mystical body of Christ." Many will say he would not have been so sanguine if writing his book after the arrival of nuclear destruction. On the contrary, Teilhard reaffirmed his early vision:

"Today, after forty years of constant reflection, it is still the same fundamental vision which I feel the need to set forth and to share, in its mature form, for the last time."[10] The fundamental vision to which he refers is *The Divine Milieu*, expressing the presence of Christ in all things.

How does Pierre Teilhard de Chardin propose that all humanity will come to be united in Christ? He does not say. He clearly is not suggesting a worldwide plan of house-to-house, neighborhood by neighborhood evangelization. Yet the faith he speaks of is an *evangelical faith* by which the world will be united and transformed in Christ. Teilhard believes that Christ will invade human hearts by flooding them with grace and love. God's plan, Teilhard insists, is firmly in place.

Such a vision of a world humanity united in Christ is not a political forecast. It is instead a mystical and prophetic foretelling of what Teilhard sees as the likely outcome of the powerful presence of Christ in the world, and also as its messianic hope. Such will be our politics, social science and economics if we entrust them to mystic scientists like Teilhard.

Karl Rahner, in envisioning a future Christian spirituality, says that "the Christian of the future will be a mystic or he or she will not exist at all." He immediately goes on to state that he is not speaking of a mysticism of singular parapsychological phenomena, but a "genuine experience of God emerging from the very heart of our existence." Faith is not a matter of pedagogic instruction, of rational argumentation and fundamental theology. No. It is, Rahner says, "the experience of God, of his Spirit, of his freedom, bursting out from the very heart of human existence and able to be really experienced there, even though this experience cannot be wholly a matter for reflection or be verbally objectified."

Rahner says that a Christian spirituality of the future has the following characteristics. First, it will be the same spirituality that the church has always had, "albeit in a mysterious identity." It will be the same, but the sameness may not look exactly the same. It will continue to be a spirituality of the Sermon on the Mount and of the evangelical counsels, in confrontation with the power structures of the world. Second, it will have to concentrate on the essentials of Christian piety, concentrated on the "ultimate data of revelation: that God exists, that we can speak to him, that his ineffable incomprehensibility is itself the very heart of our existence and consequently of our spirituality; that we can live and die with Jesus and properly with him alone in an ultimate freedom from all powers and authorities; that his incomprehensible cross is set up above our life and that this scandal reveals the true, liberating and beatifying significance of our life." Third, the spirituality of the future will not be supported by a sociologically conformist and homogeneous Christian culture; therefore, the importance of individual, personal relationships with God will emerge as an even more important factor. Fourth, fraternal community will be an essential of tomorrow's Christian practice. Fifth, it will have a "different ecclesial aspect" that is, the church will look different. This new Christian church will be less triumphalist, more ecumenical, more brotherly. This church will acknowledge its failings; it will be a church of sinners, a Pilgrim Church, continually on the way. [11]

One of the most articulate philosophers of the future is Wilfrid Desan, who in a large-scale work entitled *Planetary Man* developed a vision of the change in humanity that is necessary to forge a new world. His vision is far from utopian, but rather recognizes the flawed nature of human aspiration and endeavor. Even so, he holds up the possibility of a cosmopolis, a world city and a world citizen. This philosophical statement was published several decades ago; Desan now seems prophetic.

Reflecting on the nature of goodness, Desan says the saint is the planetary man in the realm of ethics. "This activity can be called saintly when it is noncyclical (its primary motive is not the self) nonassertive (its primary motive is not personal survival) and nonaggressive (it does not aim at the destruction of the other). Only when the individual is moving towards the welfare of the commonwealth shall we call him a saint. It is the *direction* of the mobility which counts, for it is from the trajectory that the Observer will know the missile. The absolute of the saint must be the *totum*, and it is an absolute that we shall call *uncontaminated*, since by hypothesis it is not contaminated by selfish motives in its fulfillment."

Desan defines the saint as one who cares for the other in peril without a self-serving motive—or, better said, without a motive that is entirely self-serving. Missionary zeal may be saintly when the desire to proselytize is not completely selfish:

> proselytism does not per se exclude sanctity, it may even promote it, and many missionaries have led lives of heroic charity; but it does preclude sanctity when it uses charity as the fundamental diplomacy for conversion without for that

reason making the other in peril any happier. The tacit implication, of course, is that the other will only be happy when he is as *we* are. No greater mistake could be made, for it shows a total inability to enter into the angular truth of the other, or even to suspect that there is any angularity different from ours. (Angularity is Desan's word for particularity or personal perspective, though to him it means much more.) In being a man of detachment, the saint accepts the plural and the existence of any angular behavior which does not injure the *totum*.

Desan insists that "only those who are genuinely able to rise above their own self-interest will ultimately command the respect of others. They will be revered as leaders. These are the people whose motives are believed in, who are admired and followed.

"Those who thought only of themselves the night that the Titanic hit the iceberg live in infamy, while the courageous Strausses who gave up their places in the lifeboat are universally admired."

Are ordinary people capable of such sacrificial love? Desan thinks they are. He says that saintliness "hovers over the average man—as a dream, perhaps, but not as an impossible dream."

Desan is speaking not of people in some particular fields of endeavor; not of those in occupations somehow singled out for sacrificial understanding and kindness; not at all. In fact, his very style of thought—the attempt to define humanity as "planetary man"—is predicated upon the notion that each and every individual can and must become a world-citizen; that each of us, even though bounded by angularities and singularities, is at the same time capable of living by truth.

What does this kind of holiness look like? What Desan is speaking about philosophically is saintliness that can occur in any nation or culture. "The obligation to strive towards sanctity is the obligation to strive towards the reconstruction of the One and the fulfillment of its urge to be and to survive."

Desan goes further. "Sanctity on the natural level—and no other level is of concern to us—is above all the removal, through atonement, of guilt. Hence it is natural that for our times, bowed down as we are by an immense weight of guilt, the sole means of salvation should be sanctity in action; for therein lies the expiation of the actions centered on self and the return to the oneness of the *totum* (that is, the whole).[12]

In short, men and women of outstanding virtue are needed to change the world. Because civilization is now planetary, with the attendant risk to our global environment from the escalation of technology, saintly souls are more needed than ever. But a question naturally arises with regard to the two major world religions bent upon worldwide conversion: Christianity and Islam. The hostility between these two religions appears to be escalating, just when many thinkers are calling for leaders from different cultures and nations to sit down and share their spiritualities. Can the mystics of Islam and the mystics of Christianity share faith with one another? In the present environment it seems unlikely.

Yet I find a glimmer of hope in the statement of that staunchest of Christian apologists, C. S. Lewis: "If you are a Christian you do not have to believe that all the other religions are simply wrong all the way through." Atheists, Lewis says, must believe that all the religions of the world have made one huge mistake. Christians can be more tolerant. "If you are a Christian, you are free to think that all these religions, even the queerest ones, contain at least some hint of the truth. But of course, being a Christian does mean thinking that where Christianity differs from other religions, Christianity is right and they are wrong."[13] It is a strong statement; some could view it as hidebound. I think it contains within it the germ of openness to dialogue. Prayer is a universal practice in all world religions. While ideas of God differ, or in some cases don't appear to exist at all, a great many religions are reaching for a transformed consciousness. At least three of the major world religions, Judaism, Islam and Christianity, find their origins in the prayerful journey and obedience of Abraham.

So we may perhaps hope for a world-transforming mysticism, even when we do not know how it will be carried out. The occurrence of mysticism in the world's great religions suggests that the mystics of all faiths may become a spiritual elite that leads all the rest of us to a more peaceful world. This view is subject to heated debate, for many Christian authorities insist on Christ as the unifier, even the destination (Omega Point) to which all creation is tending. As a Christian, I believe that the salvation of all humanity is accomplished in Jesus Christ. But this is a theological formulation. How will this theological formula unfold in experience? As mystics grow into deeply loving and compassionate persons, they seem to offer assurance that throughout the human race, God's saving power is at work. In any event, I am willing to state that contemplative life, which opens us up to mysticism, is a deep corrective for the headlong rush of technological modernity. Mystical prayer, contemplative prayer, lifts us to new horizons in which we can imagine more compassionate and responsible living in an uncertain world.

There are many who believe that the mystics, in all world religions, constitute an elite who will guide humanity into a more enlightened future. In one sense, this seems to be an unrealistic dream. Yet many, who are more than likely mystics, such as Mother Teresa of Calcutta, Thomas Merton and Dorothy Day, have had a profound impact on their own generations. In another sense the mystics simply serve as shining beacons to us of what the Christian formation and transformation is all about. They are lamps to our feet. Underhill calls them "expert mountaineers."[14] Following her metaphor, Harvey Egan writes: "These spiritual giants are our brothers and sisters who show us what authentic human living is and offer us paradigms for our spiritual growth."[15]

Scientists are earnestly searching for a unified theory of the universe, a "theory of everything," as they sometimes like to call it. Among their data they apparently do not include the testimony of the mystics. We, who are not astrophysicists but ordinary star-gazers may wish to allow our world view to be shaped by both Scripture and mystical writing. So in prayer and reading we may find evidence of what Paul said to the Athenians: ". . . God . . . is not far from each one of us. For 'in him we live and move and have our being'" (Acts 17:27-28).

✒ END NOTES

Chapter 1
WHAT IS MYSTICISM?

1. In great part I will be relying on Evelyn Underhill, Harvey Egan and Bernard McGinn as scholars of mysticism.

2. According to the *HarperCollins Bible Dictionary*, Paul Achtemeier, general editor, both the prophets and Paul give evidences of mysticism.

3. See Robert Ellsberg, *All Saints: Daily Reflections on Saints, Prophets and Witnesses for Our Time,* (New York: Crossroad, 1999) 414-415.

4. C. S. Lewis, *The Discarded Image,* (Cambridge, UK: Cambridge University Press, 1964) 70.

5. Other modern commentators have also taken note of first century Jewish neoplatonist influences, especially that of Philo, upon early Christian mysticism. See Harvey D. Egan, *What Are They Saying About Mysticism?* (New York: Paulist, 1982) 2.

6. William Johnston, *The Mysticism of the Cloud of Unknowing,* (New York: Fordham University Press, 2000) p. Xi.

7. Ibid, xi.

8. Some scholars tend to use the term "mystical theology" interchangeably with "mysticism." I think Thomas Corbishley does.

9. Thomas Aquinas, *De Ver.* 18:1 ad 4., as cited by Thomas Corbishley in *The New Catholic Encyclopedia,* "Mysticism," 177.

10. Augustine, *Confessions,* Book 7:23, my paraphrase. Augustine of Hippo (354–430) is considered one of the major architects of Christian thought in the West. His *Confessions* is thought to be the first spiritual autobiography.

11. Henry Vaughan, "The World," in Alexander M. Witherspoon and Frank J. Warnke, *Seventeenth-Century Prose and Poetry,* (New York: Harcourt Brace & World, 1963) 984. A footnote states that the poet is contrasting the great calm, unchanging ring of light above and the constantly revolving spheres of the Ptolemaic universe below. Vaughan goes on to read a Biblical vision into his glimpse of the universe.

12. Underhill, *Practical Mysticism,* 3.

13. Steven Katz, a contemporary scholar of comparative religion, holds this viewpoint. See Steven Katz, "Language, Epistemology, and Mysticism," pp. 22–74, in *Mysticism and Philosophical Analysis,* (New York: Oxford University Press, 1978). Cited by Harvey D. Egan in *What Are They Saying About Mysticism?*

Chapter 2
WHO CAN BE A MYSTIC?

1. C. S. Lewis, *Mere Christianity,* (New York: Macmillan, 1943) 86.

2. Underhill, *Practical Mysticism,* 1–4.

3. Ibid., 9.

4. Ron Hansen, *Mariette in Ecstasy: a Novel,* (New York: HarperCollins, 1991).

5. Mark Salzman, *Lying Awake: a Novel,* (New York: Vintage, 2001).

6. *Christian Meditation: a Letter to the Bishops of the Catholic Church on Some Aspects of Christian Meditation, the Congregation for the Doctrine of the Faith,* issued over the signatures of Joseph Cardinal Ratzinger, prefect, and Alberto Bovone, titular archbishop of Caesarea in Numidia, secretary, 15 October 1989.

7. Are all holy people mystics? Holiness, being a gift of grace, should not be hemmed in by tight limits and expectations. All holy people may not be mystics; but in my view, there is little doubt that genuine mystics are holy. Trying to pin down this equivalence is like considering the relationship between mysticism and spiritual life. All mystics practice the spiritual life; but all who practice the spiritual life are not mystics, even if they may become mystics in time to come.

8. An excellent contemporary reading of The Sermon on the Mount is given in Dallas Willard's book, *The Divine Conspiracy,* (San Francisco: HarperSanFrancisco, 1998). He consistently stresses Jesus' teaching of the availability of the kingdom.

9. Eric O. Springsted, *Simone Weil: Writings Selected with an Introduction,* (Maryknoll, NY: Orbis, 1998). I have relied on Springsted's introduction, 11–29.

10. These twelve historically practiced Christian disciplines were discussed at length by Richard J. Foster in his popular book, *A Celebration of Discipline,* (San Francisco: HarperSanFrancisco, 1979, 1988).

11. A fuller discussion of John Wesley's views on mysticism will be given in a later chapter.

12. Harvey Egan gives an extended account of Merton's idea of the hidden contemplative in *What Are They Saying About Mysticism?* (New York: Paulist Press, 1982) 58–60, and in *Christian Mysticism: the Future of a Tradition,* (New York: Pueblo Publishing, 1984) 236-237.

13. Egan, *What Are They Saying About Mysticism?* 98-99. Also see *Christian Mysticism: the Future of a Tradition,* 246-247.

Chapter 3
THE MYSTICISM OF PAUL

1. See Bernard McGinn, *The Foundations of Mysticism: Origins to the Fifth Century,* (New York: Crossroad, 1991) 69. McGinn states: "The debate about Pauline mysticism has been particularly acute in the twentieth century." McGinn evades the question, but says that the writings of Paul offer the best link between Jewish apocalypticism of the period and Christianity.

2. Cited in Emilie Griffin, ed. *Evelyn Underhill: Essential Writings,* (Maryknoll, New York: Orbis, 2003) 60.

3. See Rabbi Joseph Telushkin, *Jewish Literacy,* (New York: William Morrow and Company, 1991) 131-132.

4. See McGinn, *Foundations,* 70.

5. See "Paul the Apostle" in the *New Catholic Encyclopedia*. Volume 11, page 8. This description of Paul is given in the apocryphal Acts of Paul and derives from the legend of Paul and Thecla.

Chapter 4
EARTH'S CRAMMED WITH HEAVEN

1. Bede Griffiths, *The Golden String*, (Springfield, IL: Templegate, 1980) 9-10.

2. Evelyn Underhill, *Mysticism*, (New York: New American Library, 1955) 237.

3. William Blake, "Auguries of Innocence," in *William Blake: Selected Poetry*, (London: Penguin Books, 1988) 147.

4. Letters of William Blake, quoted in Evelyn Underhill, *Mysticism*, 235.

5. Perry Miller, ed. *Major American Writers*, (New York: Harcourt Brace, 1966) 673.

6. *Gerard Manley Hopkins: a Selection of His Poems and Prose*, W.H. Gardner, ed., 27.

7. Gerard Manley Hopkins, letter to his mother, from Balliol College, Oxford University, 22 April 1863.

8. Gardner, *Hopkins*, 51.

9. Underhill, *Mysticism*, 255

10. Elizabeth Barrett Browning, *Complete Poetical Works of Elizabeth Barrett Browning*, (Cutchogue, New York: Buccaneer Books, 1993). "Aurora Leigh," line 821, 372.

11. Attributed to Christina Rossetti.

12. Thomas Merton, *The Seven Storey Mountain*, (New York: Doubleday Image, 1970) 19.

13. See William H. Shannon *et al.*, *The Thomas Merton Encyclopedia*, (New York: Orbis Books, 2002).

14. Merton, *Entering the Silence*, 329.

15. William Shakespeare, *As You Like It*, Act II, Scene 1, Line 12.

16. Merton, *Turning Towards the World*, 312.

17. Merton, *Search for Solitude*, 190.

18. Merton, *Literary Essays*, 347.

19. Merton, *Entering the Silence*, 471.

20. Thomas Merton, "Inner Experience," 4:298, cited in *The Thomas Merton Encyclopedia*, (New York: Orbis, 2003) 321.

Chapter 5
THE SOUL'S JOURNEY

1. Muhammad Hamidullah, *Introduction to Islam*, (Paris: Centre Culturel Islamique, 1969) cited on website http//:muslimcanada.org/prophetbio.html.

2. William Wordsworth, "Ode: Intimations of Immortality from Recollections of Early Childhood," Stanza V, in David Perkins, *ed. English Romantic Writers*, (New York: Harcourt, Brace & World, 1967) 281.

3. He is not the first commentator on the Christian mystical life. According to McGinn that distinction belongs to Clement of Alexandria (died *c.* 215) who was the first to provide an extensive treatment of such ideas as vision, divinization, and union, which later were central to orthodox mysticism. McGinn does not agree with A. Levasti that Clement should be termed the "father of Christian mysticism." McGinn, *Foundations*, 101.

4. Ibid., 109.

5. These three Scriptural dimensions of the soul's journey may correspond to three aspects of spiritual transformation: the so-called purgative, illuminative, and unitive way. See discussion by Bernard McGinn and Patricia Ferris McGinn in *Early Christian Mystics: the Divine Vision of the Spiritual Masters*, (New York: Crossroad, 2003) 21–39.

6. According to Bernard McGinn in *The Foundations of Mysticism: Origins to the Fifth Century*, p. 147, Evagrius's mysticism was criticized by Hans Urs Von Balthasar, who claimed that Evagrius "stands closer to Buddhism than to Christianity." But other interpreters, including Karl Rahner and John Eudes Bamberger have given a more positive view.

7. *Practikos No. 1,* as cited in Bernard McGinn and Patricia Ferris McGinn in *Early Christian Mystics: the Divine Vision of the Spiritual Masters,* 47.

8. *On Prayer No. 3,* as cited in Bernard McGinn and Patricia Ferris McGinn in *Early Christian Mystics: the Divine Vision of the Spiritual Masters,* 55.

9. *Letter to Melania No. 6,* as cited in Bernard McGinn and Patricia Ferris McGinn in *Early Christian Mystics: the Divine Vision of the Spiritual Masters,* 54.

10. See McGinn and McGinn, *Early Christian Mystics,* 179-180.

11. Dante, *The Divine Comedy, Vol. III, Paradise,* translated by Mark Musa, (New York: Penguin Classics, 1986) p. 380, Canto XXXII, lines 139–144.

Chapter 6
THE WAY OF AFFIRMATION

1. As Harvey Egan has observed: "Merton studied the mystical traditions of both light and darkness. For him, these were basically different languages to describe an identical mystical process. Striving to reconcile the apophatic and kataphatic mystical traditions, he criticized those who focused exclusively on the former as authentic mysticism." Egan, *Christian Mysticism,* 224.

2. Brother Lawrence of the Resurrection, cited in Richard Foster, *Prayer: Finding the Heart's True Home,* (San Francisco: HarperSan Francisco, 1992) 124.

3. For a fuller discussion of Frank Laubach's life and mission, see Richard J. Foster, *Streams of Living Water,* (San Francisco: Harper SanFrancisco, 1998) 41–48.

4. Gardner, *Hopkins,* 51.

5. Ursula King, *Pierre Teilhard de Chardin: Writings,* (Maryknoll, New York: Orbis, 1999) 18.

6. Pierre Teilhard de Chardin, *The Divine Milieu,* (New York: Harper & Row, 1960) 70–79.

7. Ibid., 78.

8. Ibid., 79.

Chapter 7
THE WAY OF NEGATION

1. Jean-Pierre de Caussade, *Abandonment to Divine Providence,* John Beevers, trans., (New York, Doubleday Image, 1975), p.85. Another good translation of this work by Kitty Muggeridge has a different title: *The Sacrament of the Present Moment.* (San Francisco: HarperSanFrancisco, 1989).

2. Gregory of Nyssa, *Life of Moses,* as quoted in Denys Turner, *The Darkness of God: Negativity in Christian Mysticism,* (Cambridge, UK: Cambridge University, 1995) 17.

3. Ibid., 17.

4. Ibid., 21.

5. William Johnston, ed. *The Cloud of Unknowing and the Book of Privy Counseling,* (New York: Doubleday Image, 1973) 21.

6. Ibid., 9.

7. Ibid., 113.

8. Ibid., 136.

9. Ibid., 56.

10. The Spanish words *descalzado and descalzo* mean barefooted. (See *Casell's Spanish-English Dictionary,* New York: Macmillan, 1968). Discalced Carmelites do, however, wear sandals, as is noted in the description of Brother Lawrence's duties as a sandalmaker in his monastery.

11. Kieran Kavanaugh, O.C.D., ed., *John of the Cross: Selected Writings,* (New York: Paulist Press, 1987) from "The Ascent to Mount Carmel," 63.

12. Ibid., 102.

Chapter 8
TRACING THE MYSTIC PATH

1. Underhill, *Mysticism*, 91-92.

2. Thomas of Celano, *Legenda Prima*, cap. I, cited in Underhill, *Mysticism*, 180.

3. Griffin, *Turning: Reflections on the Experience of Conversion*, (New York: Doubleday, 1980, 1982).

4. C. S. Lewis, *Surprised by Joy: The Shape of My Early Life*, (New York: Harcourt Brace Janovich, 1955) 214.

5. Underhill, *Mysticism*, 196.

6. Ibid., 197.

7. Ibid., 201.

8. Ibid., 204.

9. Ibid.

10. Ibid., 205.

11. Ibid., 208

12. C. S. Lewis, *The Four Loves*, (New York: Harcourt Brace & World, 1960) 166. Also see his essay, "First and Second Things," included in Walter Hooper, ed., C. S. Lewis, *First and Second Things*, (London: Collins/Fount Paperbacks, 1985).

13. Underhill, *Mysticism*, 216.

14. Ibid. 348. This comment suggests that for Underhill, the *via negativa* is the primary mystical path. As we have noted, Harvey Egan and others would question that.

15. Ibid, 395.

16. Ibid., 396.

17. Ibid., 258

18. Emilie Griffin, *Clinging: the Experience of Prayer*, (San Francisco: HarperSanFrancisco, 1984; Wichita, Kansas: Eighth Day Books, 2003).

19. Also *dvekut*. See Herbert Weiner, *9½ Mystics: The Kabbala Today*, (New York: Macmillan, 1969, 1992) 65.

20. Underhill, *Mysticism*, 264-265.

21. Ibid., 335.

22. Ibid., 348.

23. Ibid., 446.

24. Ibid., 450.

Chapter 9
THE LOVE LANGUAGE OF MYSTICISM

1. Henry Chadwick, trans., *Saint Augustine Confessions*, (Oxford University Press, 1991) 201.

2. M. L. del Mastro, trans., Juliana of Norwich, *Revelations of Divine Love*, (New York: Doubleday, 1977) 134-135, abridged.

3. Rosamund S. Allen, ed., *Richard Rolle: the English Writings*, (New York: Paulist Press, 1988) 63.

4. John Frederick Nims, trans., *The Poems of John of the Cross: A Bilingual Edition*, (Chicago: University of Chicago Press, Midway Reprint Edition 1989) 19–21. Another translation offers:

> One dark night
> Fired with love's urgent longings
> —Ah, the sheer grace!—
> I went out unseen
> My house being now all stilled.

5. *John of the Cross: Selected Writings*, (New York: Paulist Press, 1987) "The Ascent of Mount Carmel," 55.

6. Another translation reads:

> O lamps of fire
> In whose splendors
> The deep caverns of feeling
> Once obscure and blind
> Now give forth, so rarely, so exquisitely,
> Both warmth and light to their beloved.

7. Ibid., 23.

8. Tessa Bielecki, ed., *Teresa of Avila: Mystical Writings,* (New York: Crossroad, 1994) 147.

9. *Seventeenth-Century Prose and Poetry,* 2nd ed., edited by Alexander M. Witherspoon and Frank J. Warnke, (New York: Harcourt Brace & World, 1963) 757.

10. Witherspoon and Warnke, *Seventeenth Century Prose and Poetry,* 850. I have omitted the second to last verse of Herbert's poem, entitled "Matins."

11. William Blake, "The Little Black Boy," stanza 4, in William Blake, *Selected Poetry,* (New York: Penguin, 1988) 24.

12. William Blake, *Selected Poetry,* 29.

13. Patricia O'Connor, *The Inner Life of Therese of Lisieux,* (Huntington, Indiana: Our Sunday Visitor, 1997) 155–156.

14. See Richard J. Foster, *Prayer: Finding the Heart's True Home.* (San Francisco: HarperSanFrancisco, 1992).

Chapter 10
MYSTICAL GIFTS AND UNUSUAL PHENOMENA

1. This story is told more fully in *Butler's Lives of the Saints*: Concise Edition, (San Francisco: Harper & Row, 1985) 43. The story is attributed to St. Gregory.

2. Quoted by Evelyn Underhill. See, Emilie Griffin, ed., *Evelyn Underhill: Essential Writings,* (Maryknoll, NY: Orbis, 2003) 71.

3. Ibid., 71.

4. Herbert Thurston, S.J., *The Physical Phenomena of Mysticism,* (London: Burns Oates, 1952) 7.

5. Ibid., 10–11.

6. Ibid., 9–18.

7. Harnett, "The Strange Case of Therese Neumann," Part I of a four-part series, available on the internet at www.bonsai-east.com/rarebird/neuman1.htm. Originally published as *Therese Neumann—Saint or Psycho?*

8. Thurston, 385–387.

9. *Selected Letters of St. Ignatius Loyola, #28* To Father Nicholas Goudanus, "On the Gift of Tears," Rome, November 22, 1553. This translation of Ignatius's letter appears in William Griffin, *Thomas à Kempis: Consolations for My Soul,* (New York: Crossroad/Carlisle, 2003) 195-196.

Chapter 11
GROUP MYSTICISM

1. Al and Patti Mansfield have given a full account of the Louisiana Charismatic Renewal in their essay, "New Manifestations of the Spirit: The Origin and Early Impact of the Catholic Charismatic Renewal in Louisiana," which appears in pp. 433–448 of Glenn Conrad, ed., *Cross, Crozier and Crucible: A Volume Celebrating the Bicentennial of a Catholic Diocese in Louisiana,* (New Orleans: Archdiocese of New Orleans, 1992). I was the editor of the section in which their essay appears.

2. Richard J. Foster and Emilie Griffin, editors and compilers, *Spiritual Classics: Readings for Individuals and Groups,* (San Francisco: HarperSanFrancisco, 1999) 132.

3. *The Journal of George Fox* edited by John L. Nickalls (Cambridge: Cambridge University Press, 1952). Reprinted with corrections, London: London Yearly Meeting, 1986. Fox's *Journal* is a prototype of the modern religious journal: insightful, powerful, compassionate.

4. *The Journal of George Fox,* as cited in Richard J. Foster and Emilie Griffin, eds., *Spiritual Classics: Selected Readings for Individuals and Groups on the Twelve Spiritual Disciplines,* (San Francisco: HarperSanFrancisco, 2000) 128-129.

5. Ibid., 130.

6. John Marks Templeton and Kenneth Seeman Giniger, eds. *Spiritual Evolution: Scientists Discuss Their Beliefs*, (Templeton Foundation Press) 1998.

7. From Francois Fenelon, *Christian Perfection,* cited in Richard J. Foster, *Freedom of Simplicity,* (San Francisco: Harper & Row Publishers, 1981) 101.

8. See Robert G. Tuttle, Jr., *Mysticism in the Wesleyan Tradition,* (Grand Rapids, MI: Zonder van/Francis Asbury Press, 1989) 149.

9. Jeanne Marie Guyon, generally referred to as Madame Guyon (1648–1717) was a controversial spiritual writer, at the heart of the Quietist controversy.

10. Tuttle, Jr., *Mysticism in the Wesleyan Tradition,* 149.

11. Introduction by Frank Whaling to *John and Charles Wesley: Selected Writings and Hymns,* (New York: Paulist Press, 1981) 10. Frank Whaling is also editor of this volume.

12. Merton, *Seven Storey Mountain,* (New York: Doubleday Image, 1970.)

13. Merton, *Seeking Paradise,* Paul Pearson, ed., (Maryknoll, New York: Orbis, 2003) 49–53.

14. See "Dervishes," by P. K. Hitti, in *The New Catholic Encyclopedia,* Vol. 4, 783.

Chapter 12
A MYSTICISM OF EVERYDAY LIFE

1. Kamenetz, *The Jew in the Lotus: a Poet's Rediscovery of Jewish Identity in Buddhist India,* (San Francisco, HarperSanFrancisco, 1994) 75. A second exploration of modern Jewish spirituality by the same author is *Stalking Elijah: Adventures with Today's Jewish Mystical Masters* (San Francisco: HarperSanFrancisco, 1998). Kamenetz is on the creative writing faculty at Louisiana State University in Baton Rouge. He lives in New Orleans.

2. For a good account of the Lubavitch sect, see Weiner, ibid., 155–196.

3. Kamenetz, 301.

4. Ibid., 77.

5. Ibid., 72.

6. Ibid., 191-197.

7. Karl Rahner, *Theological Investigations 3*, (Baltimore, MD: Helicon, 1973) 279.

8. Hugo Rahner, "Study and Daily Life," in Hugo and Karl Rahner, *Prayers for Meditation*, (New York: Herder and Herder, 1962) 54.

9. Brother Lawrence of the Resurrection, *The Practice of the Presence of God*, translated by Salvatore Sciurba, OCD, (Washington, DC: ICS Publications, 1993) 52.

10. Ibid., 53.

11. Ibid., 43.

12. Some works attributed to Brother Alphonsus, it later turned out, were not really his. Those that he did actually write himself were awkward, repetitive, and lacking in style. To make matters worse, he is often confused with Father Alonso Rodriguez, (1526-1616) also a Spaniard and the author of *Christian Perfection*, who was never canonized.

13. Gerard Manley Hopkins, "In honor of St. Alphonsus Rodriguez," in *Gerard Manley Hopkins: A Selection of His Poetry and Prose*, (Harmondsworth, Middlesex, England: Penguin, 1963) 66-67.

Chapter 13
WORLD-TRANSFORMING MYSTICISM

1. Preface by Morton Kelsey to Paul Marechal, *Dancing Madly Backwards: A Journey into God*, (New York: Crossroad, 1982) xi.

2. C. S. Lewis, *The Last Battle*, (New York, Macmillan, 1970) 170-171.

3. Paul Marechal, *Dancing Madly Backwards: A Journey into God*, see chapter 7, "In the Heart of a Great Round Dance."

4. John Donne, "Devotions Upon Emergent Occasions, XVII. Meditation," in Alexander M. Witherspoon and Frank J. Warnke,

Seventeenth Century Prose and Poetry, (New York: Harcourt, Brace & World, 1963) 68.

5. Pierre Teilhard de Chardin, *The Divine Milieu*, 114-115.

6. Ibid., 114.

7. Ibid., 136.

8. Ibid., 124.

9. Ibid., 124.

10. Ibid.,139. An appendix to the original book was added by the editor, quoting from written remarks made by Teilhard in 1955.

11. Karl Rahner, *The Practice of Faith: a Handbook of Contemporary Spirituality*, (New York: Crossroad, 1983) in "The Spirituality of the Future," 18–26.

12. Wilfrid Desan, *The Planetary Man*, (New York: Macmillan, 1972) 38, 372.

13. C. S. Lewis, "The Rival Conceptions of God," in *Mere Christianity*, (New York: Macmillan, 1981) 31.

14. Underhill, *Mysticism*, 448.

15. Egan, *What Are They Saying About Mysticism?* 49.

⌐ SELECTED BIBLIOGRAPHY

_____. *The Cloud of Unknowing*. Edited, with an Introduction by James Walsh, SJ. Preface by Simon Tugwell, OP. New York: Paulist Press, 1981.

Augustine of Hippo. *Confessions*. Translated by Henry Chadwick. New York: Oxford University Press, 1991.

Barry, SJ, William A. *Finding God in All Things: A Companion to the Spiritual Exercises of St. Ignatius*. Notre Dame IN: Ave Maria Press, 1991.

_____ and Robert G. Doherty, SJ, *Contemplatives in Action: The Jesuit Way*. New York: Paulist, 2002.

Bernard of Clairvaux. *Selected Works*. New York: Paulist Press, 1987.

Blake, William. *Selected Poetry*. Edited by W. H. Stevenson. New York: Penguin Books, 1988.

Browning, Elizabeth Barrett. *Complete Poetical Works*. Cutchogue NY: Buccaneer Books, 1993.

Clément, Olivier. *The Roots of Christian Mysticism: Texts and Commentary*. Hyde Park NY: New City Press, 1993 (1982).

Congregation for the Doctrine of the Faith. *Letter to the Bishops of the Catholic Church on Some Aspects of Christian Meditation*. Vatican City, 1989. Washington DC: Office for Publishing and Promotion Services, United States Catholic Conference, 1989.

Dante Alighieri, *The Divine Comedy*. Volume III: *Paradise*. Translated with an Introduction by Mark Musa. New York: Viking Penguin, 1986 (1984).

De Caussade, SJ, Jean-Pierre. *Abandonment to Divine Providence*. Translated and introduced by John Beevers. New York: Doubleday Image, 1975.

Desan, Wilfrid. *Planetary Man*. New York: Macmillan, 1960.

De Rougemont, Denis. *Love in the Western World*. Translated by Montgomery Belgion. Revised and augmented edition. New York: Harper Colophon, 1974 (1940).

De Waal, Esther. *The Way of Simplicity: The Cistercian Tradition*. Maryknoll NY: Orbis Books, 1998.

Dickinson, Emily. *Selected Letters and Poems of Emily Dickinson*. New York: Doubleday, 1959.

Donne, John. *The Complete Poetry and Selected Prose of John Donne*. New York: The Modern Library, Random House, 1952.

Dupré, Louis and James A. Wiseman OSB, editors. *Light from Light: An Anthology of Christian Mysticism*. New York: Paulist Press, 1988.

Dupré, Louis. *Religious Mystery and Rational Reflection: Excursions in the Phenomenology and Philosophy of Religion*. Grand Rapids, Michigan: William B. Eerdmans, 1998. See especially his essay on "The Experience of Mystical Union in Western Religion."

Eckhart, Meister. *The Essential Sermons, Commentaries, Treatises and Defense*. New York: Paulist Press, 1981.

Egan, SJ, Harvey D. *Christian Mysticism: The Future of a Tradition*. New York: Pueblo Publishing, 1984.

_____. *The Spiritual Exercises and the Ignatian Mystical Horizon*. Foreword by Karl Rahner, SJ. St. Louis MO: Institute of Jesuit Sources, 1976.

_____. *What Are They Saying About Mysticism?* New York: Paulist Press, 1982.

Eliot, T.S. *Collected Poems, 1909-1962*. New York: Harcourt, Brace, & World, 1963.

Ellsberg, Robert, compiler and editor. *All Saints: Daily Reflections on Saints, Prophets, and Witnesses for Our Time*. New York: Crossroad, 1999.

Fadiman, James and Robert Frager, editors. *Essential Sufism*. Foreword by Huston Smith. Edison NJ: Castle Books, 1998 (1997).

Fine, Lawrence, translator. *Safed Spiritualiy: Rules of Mystical Piety, The Beginning of Wisdom*. Preface by Louis Jacobs. New York: Paulist Press, 1984.

Francis and Clare: the Complete Works, translation and introduction by Regis Armstrong, OFM, Cap., and Ignatius C. Brady, OFM. New York: Paulist Press, 1982.

Foster, Richard J. *Celebration of Discipline: The Path to Spiritual Growth.* Revised edition. San Francisco: HarperSanFrancisco, 1988 (1979).

_____. *Freedom of Simplicity.* San Francisco: HarperSanFrancisco, 1981.

_____. *Prayer: Finding the Heart's True Home.* San Francisco: HarperSanFrancisco, 1992.

_____. *Streams of Living Water: Celebrating the Great Traditions of Christian Faith.* Foreword by Martin Marty. San Francisco: HarperSan Francisco, 1998.

Foster, Richard J. and Emilie Griffin, compilers and editors. *Spiritual Classics: Readings for Individuals and Groups.* San Francisco: HarperSan Francisco, 1999.

Fox, George. *The Journal of George Fox.* Edited by John L. Nickalls. Cambridge: Cambridge University Press, 1952.

Fremantle, Anne and Christopher, editors and translators. *In Love with Love: 100 of the Greatest Mystical Poems.* New York: Paulist Press, 1978.

Gregory of Nyssa, *The Life of Moses.* New York: Paulist Press, 1978.

Griffin, Emilie. *Clinging: The Experience of Prayer.* Wichita KS: Eighth Day Books, 2003 (1983).

_____. *Turning: Reflections on the Experience of Conversion.* New York: Doubleday, 1980.

Griffiths, OSB, Bede. *The Golden String: An Autobiography.* Springfield IL: Templegate, 1980 (1954).

Guiley, Rosemary Ellen. *Harper's Encyclopedia of Mystical and Paranormal Experience.* Introduction by Marion Zimmer Bradley. San Francisco: HarperSanFrancisco, 1991.

Hamidullah, Muhammad. *Introduction to Islam.* Paris: Centre Culturel Islamique, 1969.

Hansen, Ron. *Mariette in Ecstasy: A Novel.* New York: HarperCollins, 1991.

Herbert, George. *The Works of George Herbert*. Edited with a Commentary by F. E. Hutchinson. Oxford UK: Clarendon Press, 1941.

Herbstrith, OCD, Waltraud. *Never Forget: Christian and Jewish Perspectives on Edith Stein*. Translated by Susanne Batzdorff. Washington DC: Institute of Carmelite Studies, 1998.

Hopkins, SJ, Gerard Manley. *Gerard Manley Hopkins: A Selection of His Poems and Prose*. Compiled and edited by W. H. Gardner. Baltimore MD: Penguin Books, 1953.

Ignatius of Loyola, *Spiritual Exercises*. Edited and translated by Anthony Mottola. New York: Doubleday, 1989.

James, William. *Varieties of Religious Experience*. New York: Macmillan, 1961.

John of the Cross. *The Poems of John of the Cross: A Bilingual Edition*. Translated by John Frederick Nims. Chicago: University of Chicago Press, Midway Reprint Edition, 1989.

_____. *Selected Writings*. Edited with an Introduction by Kieran Kavanaugh, OCD. New York: Paulist Press, 1987.

Johnston, SJ, William. *Mystical Theology: The Science of Love*. Maryknoll NY: Orbis Books, 1995.

_____. *The Cloud of Unknowing and the Book of Privy Counseling*. New York: Doubleday Image, 1973.

_____. *The Mysticism of the Cloud of Unknowing*. New York: Fordham University Press, 2000.

_____. *The Wounded Stag: Christian Mysticism Today*. New York: Fordham University Press, 1998.

Jones, Timothy. *The Art of Prayer: A Simple Guide*. New York: Ballantine, 1997.

Jones, Rufus. *Essential Writings*. Selected and with an Introduction by Kerry Walters. Maryknoll NY: Orbis Books, 2001.

Julian of Norwich. *Revelations of Divine Love*. Translated by M. L. del Mastro. New York: Doubleday, 1977.

Kamenetz, Rodger. *The Jew in the Lotus: A Poet's Rediscovery of Jewish Identity in Buddhist India*. San Francisco: HarperSanFrancisco,1994.

_____. *The Lowercase Jew: Poems.* Evanston IL: Northwestern University Press, 2003.

_____. *Stalking Elijah: Adventures with Today's Jewish Mystical Masters.* San Francisco: HarperSan Francisco, 1997.

Katz, Steven T. ed., *Mysticism and Philosophical Analysis.* New York: Oxford University Press, 1978. See his essay, "Language, Epistemology, and Mysticism," 22–74.

Kelly, Thomas R. *A Testament of Devotion.* San Francisco: HarperSan Francisco, 1996.

Kempis, Thomas à. *The Imitation of Christ.* Translated by William Griffin. San Francisco: HarperSanFrancisco, 2000.

_____. *Consolations for My Soul.* Translated by William Griffin. New York: Crossroad, 2004.

Laubach, Frank. *Letters by a Modern Mystic.* Syracuse, New York: New Readers Press, 1979.

Lawrence of the Resurrection, Brother. *The Practice of the Presence of God.* Critical Edition. Translated by Salvatore Sciurba, OCD. Foreword by Gerald G. May. Washington DC: Institute of Carmelite Studies, 1994.

Lewis, C. S. *The Discarded Image: An Introduction to Medieval and Renaissance Literature.* Cambridge: Cambridge University Press, 1964.

_____. *First and Second Things: Essays on Theology and Ethics.* London: Colins Fount, 1985.

_____. *The Four Loves.* New York: Harcourt, Brace & World, 1960.

_____. *Mere Christianity.* Edited and with an Introduction by Walter Hooper. New York: Macmillan, 1981 (1952).

_____. *Surprised by Joy: The Shape of My Life.* New York: Harcourt, Brace, and World, 1955.

Louf, OCSO, André. *Teach Us to Pray: Learning a Little about God.* New York: Paulist 1975, (1974).

Loyola, S.J., Ignatius. *Fifty Selected Letters of St. Ignatius of Loyola.* Woodstock Theological Library Jesuit Texts, www.georgetown.edu/centers/woodstock/ignatius/Jesuit_texts.htm

Luke, Helen M. *Dark Wood to White Rose: Journey and Transformation in Dante's Divine Comedy.* New York: Parabola Books, 1989.

Marechal, Paul. *Dancing Madly Backwards: A Journey into God.* Foreword by Morton Kelsey. New York: Crossroad, 1982.

May, Gerald. *The Dark Night of the Soul: A Psychiatrist Explores the Connection between Darkness and Spiritual Growth.* San Francisco: HarperSanFrancisco, 2004.

McGinn, Bernard. *The Foundations of Mysticism: Origins to the Fifth Century.* New York: Crossroad, 1981.

_____ and Patricia Ferris McGinn. *Early Christian Mystics: The Divine Vision of the Spiritual Masters.* New York: Crossroad, 2003.

McGuckin, John Anthony, compiler and translator. *The Book of Mystical Chapters: Meditations on the Soul's Ascent from the Desert Fathers and Other Early Christian Contemplatives.* Boston: Shambhala, 2002.

Merton, Thomas. *Contemplation in a World of Action.* New York: Doubleday, 1971.

_____. *Contemplative Prayer.* New York: Herder and Herder, 1969.

_____. *Entering the Silence: Becoming a Monk and Writer.* The Journals of Thomas Merton, Volume 2: 1941-1952. Edited by Jonathan Montaldo. San Francisco: HarperSanFrancisco, 1996.

_____. *The Inner Experience.* Unpublished manuscript, 1959, 1968.

_____. *Literary Essays.* Edited by Patrick Hart. New York: New Directions, 1981.

_____. *Mystics and Zen Masters.* New York: Farrar, Straus and Giroux, 1967.

_____. *New Seeds of Contemplation.* New York: New Directions, 1962.

_____. *A Search for Solitude: Pursuing the Monk's True Life.* The Journals of Thomas Merton, Volume 3: 1952-1960. San Francisco: HarperSanFrancisco, 1996.

_____. *Seeking Paradise.* Edited by Paul Pearson. Maryknoll NY: Orbis Books, 2003.

_____. *The Seven Storey Mountain*. New York: Harcourt, Brace, and World, 1948.

_____. *Turning Toward the World*. San Francisco: HarperSanFrancisco, 1997.

Nouwen, Henri J. M.. *The Genesee Diary*. New York: Image Books, 1981.

_____. *The Way of the Heart: Desert Spirituality and Contemporary Ministry*. San Francisco: HarperSanFrancisco, 1981.

O'Connor, Patricia. *The Inner Life of Therese of Lisieux*. Huntington IN: Our Sunday Visitor Press, 1997.

Otto, Rudolf. *The Idea of the Holy*. New York: Oxford University Press, 1958.

Quaker Spirituality: Selected Writings. Edited and introduced by Douglas V. Steere. Preface by Douglas V. Steere and Elizabeth Gray Vining. New York: Paulist Press, 1984.

Rahner, S.J., Karl. *The Practice of Faith: A Handbook of Contemporary Spirituality*. New York: Crossroad, 1983.

Rahner, S.J., Hugo and Karl. *Prayers for Meditation*. New York: Herder & Herder, 1962.

Reinhold, H. A., editor. *The Soul Afire: Revelations of the Mystics*. New York: Doubleday Image, 1973.

Richard Rolle. *The English Writings*. Translated, edited, and introduced by Rosamund S. Allen. Preface by Valerie M. Lagorio. New York: Paulist Press, 1988.

Rohr, Richard. *Everything Belongs: The Gift of Contemplative Prayer*. New York: Crossroad, 2003.

Rumi, Jalal al-Din. *The Illustrated Rumi: A Treasury of Wisdom from the Poet of the Soul*. San Francisco: HarperSan Francisco, 2000.

Salzman, Mark. *Lying Awake: A Novel*. New York: Vintage, 2001.

Shannon, William H., Christine M. Bochen, Patrick F. O'Connell, compilers and editors. *The Thomas Merton Encyclopedia*. Maryknoll NY: Orbis Books, 2002.

The Shakers: Two Centuries of Spiritual Reflection. Edited by Robley Edward Whitson. New York: Paulist Press, 1983.

Stein, Edith. *Selected Writings.* With Comments, Reminiscences, and Translations of her Prayers and Poems by her Niece, Susanne M. Batzdorff. Springfield IL: Templegate, 1990.

Tamburello, OFM, Dennis. *Ordinary Mysticism.* With an Introduction by Bernard McGinn. New York: Paulist Press, 1996.

Teilhard de Chardin SJ, Pierre. *The Divine Milieu: An Essay on the Interior Life.* New York: Harper & Row, 1960 (1957).

_____. *The Hymn of the Universe.* New York: Harper & Row, 1965.

_____. *Writings.* Compiled and edited by Ursula King. Maryknoll NY: Orbis Books, 1999.

Teresa of Avila. *The Interior Castle.* Translation by Kieran Kavanaugh, OCD, and Otilio Rodriguez, OCD. Introduction by Kieran Kavanaugh, OCD. Preface by Raimundo Pannikar. New York: Paulist Press, 1979.

_____. *Teresa of Avila: Mystical Writings.* Compiled and edited by Tessa Bielecki. New York: Crossroad, 1994.

Therese of Lisieux, *The Story of a Soul: The Autobiography of Therese of Lisieux.* Translated by John Clarke, OCD. Washington, D.C.: Institute of Carmelite Studies, 1996.

Thurston, SJ, Herbert. *The Physical Phenomena of Mysticism.* Edited by J. H. Crehan, SJ. London: Burns Oates, 1952.

Tuoti, Frank X. *The Dawn of the Mystical Age: An Invitation to Enlightenment.* New York: Crossroad, 1997.

Turner, Denys. *The Darkness of God: Negativity in Christian Mysticism.* Cambridge: Cambridge University Press, 1995.

Tuttle Jr., Robert G. *Mysticism in the Wesleyan Tradition.* Foreword by William R. Canon. Grand Rapids MI: Francis Asbury Press, 1989.

Underhill, Evelyn. *Mysticism: A Study in the Nature and Development of Man's Spiritual Consciousness.* New York: New American Library, 1955 (1910).

_____. *Mystics of the Church.* Cambridge UK: James Clarke, 1975 (1925).

_____. *The Mystic Way: A Psychological Study in Christian Origins.* London: J. M. Dent, 1913.

_____. *Practical Mysticism: A Little Book for Normal People.* New York: Dutton, 1914.

_____. *Essential Writings.* Selected with an Introduction by Emilie Griffin. Maryknoll: Orbis Books, 2003.

Von Balthasar, Hans Urs. *Prayer.* San Franscisco: Ignatius Press, 1986.

Von Hugel, Friedrich. *The Mystical Element of Religion:* 2 vol study of Catherine of Genoa. London: J. M. Dent, James Clarke and Co., 1961.

Ward, SLG, Benedicta. *The Wisdom of the Desert Fathers.* SLG Press, Convent of the Incarnation, Fairacres, Oxford, England, 1977.

Weil, Simone. *Waiting for God.* Translated by E. Crauford. New York: Harper & Row, 1973.

_____. *Writings.* Selected with an Introduction by Eric O. Springsted. Maryknoll NY: Orbis Books, 1998.

Telushkin, Joseph. *Jewish Literacy.* New York: Morrow, 1991.

Weiner, Herbert. *9½ Mystics: The Kabbala Today.* New and expanded edition. Foreword by Eli Wiesel. Afterword by Adin Steinsalz. With a New Coda by the Author. New York: Macmillan, 1992 (1969).

Wesley, John and Charles. *Selected Writings and Hymns.* Edited, with an Introduction by Frank Whaling. New York: Paulist Press, 1981.

Willard, Dallas. *The Divine Conspiracy: Rediscovering Our Hidden Life in God.* San Francisco: HarperSanFrancisco, 1998.

Woods, OP, Richard. *Mysticism and Prophecy: The Dominican Tradition.* Maryknoll NY: Orbis Books, 1998.

Zohar, The Book of Enlightenment. Translation and Introduction by Daniel Chanan Matt. Preface by Arthur Green. New York: Paulist Press, 1983.

Wonderful and Dark Is This Road ✒